Contents

FOREWORD

A concern for the ethical instruction and formation of students has always been a part of American higher education. Yet that concern has by no means been uniform or free of controversy. The centrality of moral philosophy in the undergraduate curriculum during the mid-nineteenth century gave way later during that century to the first signs of increasing specialization of the disciplines. By the middle of the twentieth century, instruction in ethics had, by and large, become confined almost exclusively to departments of philosophy and religion. Efforts to introduce ethics teaching in the professional schools and elsewhere in the university often met with indifference or outright hostility.

The past decade has seen a remarkable resurgence of interest in the teaching of ethics at both the undergraduate and professional school levels. Beginning in 1977, The Hastings Center, with the support of the Rockefeller Brothers Fund and the Carnegie Corporation of New York, undertook a systematic study of the teaching of ethics in American higher education. Our concern focused on the extent and quality of that teaching, and on the main possibilities and problems posed by widespread efforts to find a more central and significant role for ethics in the curriculum.

As part of that project, a number of papers, studies, and monographs were commissioned. Moreover, in an attempt to gain some degree of consensus, the authors of those studies worked together as a group for a period of two years. The study presented here represents one outcome of the project. We hope and believe it will be helpful for those concerned to advance and deepen the teaching of ethics in higher education.

Daniel Callahan   Sissela Bok
Project Co-Directors
The Hastings Center
Project on the Teaching of Ethics

About the Author

Lawrence W. Sherman, Director of Research of the Police Foundation, has directed research projects on police corruption, police use of deadly force, higher education for police officers, police responses to domestic violence, and misconduct by organizations. His books include *Scandal and Reform*, *Police Corruption*, *The Quality of Police Education*, and *Police and Violence*. He is on leave from the State University of New York at Albany where he is an associate professor of criminal justice.

Preface

In 1978, the Police Foundation's National Advisory Commission on Higher Education for Police Officers recommended that "every police education program should include in its required curriculum a thorough consideration of the value choices and ethical dilemmas of police work" (Sherman, et al., 1978:89). That recommendation was part of a larger report calling for more liberal education and relatively less technical training in the preparation of police officers. The report created a widespread controversy among the more than 1,000 college-level degree programs in criminology and criminal justice. But the specific recommendation concerning ethical education was rarely challenged, not even in the more than thirty critical commentaries on the report that the Police Foundation later published (Police Foundation, 1979).

A subsequent Commission representing the two major academic associations in the field, the Academy of Criminal Justice Sciences and the American Society of Criminology, was established in 1979 to continue to review the nature and quality of higher education in this area. Funded by a grant from the Law Enforcement Assistance Administration of the U.S. Department of Justice, the new Joint Commission on Criminology and Criminal Justice Education and Standards funded the preparation of a series of studies of the key issues it faced, including the present work. Originally published by the Commission itself under the title, "The Teaching of Ethics in Criminology and Criminal Justice," this version reflects moderately substantial alterations. The alterations are based largely on the very helpful comments of several people affiliated with the Hastings Center: Daniel Callahan, Ruth Macklin, Sissela Bok, and Arthur Caplan. Professor Jeffrey Reiman of the American University School of Justice also offered very detailed comments.

The reactions of these philosophers have helped me make the presentation fit the Hastings Center's series on the Teaching of Ethics in Higher Education. Publication of the monograph in this series helps it to reach an audience that the Joint Commission on Criminology and Criminal Justice Education and Standards is less well situated to reach: those people, outside the fields of criminology and criminal justice, who are responsible for the general governance of higher education. For as academic leaders give more consideration to the teaching of ethics generally, it is critically important that the role of ethics in crime-related education not be overlooked. Dr. Richard A. Ward, project director of the Joint Commission and vice-chancellor of the University of Illinois in Chicago, deserves special thanks for agreeing to this joint publication arrangement. Dr. Vincent Webb, former project director of the commission, deserves thanks for encouraging the idea for the monograph and for tolerating its tardy production.

This monograph can also be considered the first in a series of efforts by the Police Foundation to implement the rcommendation on ethics of its national commission on police education. The foundation has also estabished its own Institute of Police Ethics, directed by Dr. Frederick Elliston. Under a grant from the National Endowment for the Humanities, the Institute is currently surveying college programs and police academies to find out more about how much and what kind of coverage ethics receives in police education. The foundation is also continuing a project begun by the Hastings Center on the ethics of deception in police undercover investigations, such as "Abscam."

Many people have contributed to the original writing of this monograph. Most important are Herman Goldstein, whose discussion of goal conflicts in police work (Goldstein, 1977) laid out the challenge for someone to address these issues; Daniel Callahan, Sissela Bok, and the other authors of The Hastings Center Report, *The Teaching of Ethics in Higher Education*, from which I borrow frequently and unashamedly; Frederick Elliston, my colleague at SUNY-Albany and the moral philosopher half of our team-taught course and forthcoming book in police ethics; the many bright and articulate students in that course; and (not the least) my parents, Donald and Margaret Sherman, who tried their best to make me a moral person. I thank them all.

L. W. Sherman

I. The Need for Ethics

Few vocations offer as much moral complexity as criminal justice. Few occupations are as ethically demanding or as full of moral conflicts. No other occupation requires its members to make moral judgments about how other people have behaved, and then to make and implement moral judgments about how society should respond to them. No other occupation is legally empowered with the discretion to kill people on that basis.

In 1976, American police officers, at their own discretion, killed an estimated 600 people (Sherman, 1980 b). Judges and juries sentenced several hundred others to death. Several million other people were arrested. Most were let go without serious punishment. The agents of criminal justice decided whether, and how severely, the society should punish people whose immoral conduct ranged from brutal rape-murders to public intoxication. Measured solely by the volume of moral confrontations and judgments, it would seem that the moral boundaries of our society are set not by organized religion, not by the schools, but by the agents of criminal justice.

Yet it is hard to find an occupation so poorly prepared for its moral tasks. Many, if not most, criminal justice agents obtain their positions with only a high school education. Their training academies' curriculum, until recently, has been wholly lacking in any consideration of ethics. Partly for this reason, the criminal justice study commissions of the late 1960s and early 1970s recommended more recruitment of college-educated people to become police, parole, and corrections officers (see Sherman, et al., 1978). The premise of this recommendation was that college education would provide a broader preparation for all aspects of criminal justice work, including its moral decisionmaking. But given our still limited knowledge about the current state of ethics teaching in criminal justice higher education, that premise would seem to be incorrect. For at the present time, there is relatively little explicit teaching of ethics in criminal justice departments.

Not all college graduates who work in criminal justice major in that field, nor are they required to, except in a few jurisdictions. But there is some evidence that the academic field of criminal justice (or a similar name, such as criminology or police administration) is the most common major among police officers (Hoover, 1976). It is reasonable to suspect the same is true of corrections and probation officers who attend college. So although the moral education of criminal justice officials includes many disciplines, it is the new field of criminal justice (barely a decade old) that has the greatest opportunity and responsibility for that moral education.

A. The Purpose of the Study

This study explores that opportunity. Its purpose is to show why and how criminal justice education could undertake more *explicit* teaching of ethics, as distinct from the implied consideration of value problems under the guise of fact. Thus it raises six questions, each considered in a separate chapter.

1. Why is ethics needed in criminal justice education?

At a time of contraction in higher education, ethics may seem like an expensive frill that criminal justice programs can do without. Given the traditional views of criminal justice teaching as providing either technical skills or social science explanations and descriptions, or both, the need for ethics is not readily apparent. But a reconsideration of the relationship between the nature of criminal justice work and the curriculum in criminal justice education suggests that ethics needs to be a basic part of that curriculum.

2. What should be the specific aims of teaching ethics in criminal justice education?

The ancient problem of whether virtue can be taught need not cripple ethics in criminal justice education. Much more modest goals are nonetheless worthwhile, such as teaching the reasoning process for arriving at moral decisions. An ethics course need not be judged solely, or at all, by the actual behavior of its graduates, but rather by the quality of their learning.

3. How can ethics be fitted into the structures of existing curricula?

Even if the need for ethics is accepted, there are many practical problems presented by an attempt to fit ethics in. Teaching one main course on ethics, rather than teaching a little ethics in every course, is one of the major choices. If ethics is to be taken seriously, teaching it as a separate course seems to be the only viable option.

4. What is the scope of ethical problems of criminal justice?

The list of problems is potentially endless, but it is important to begin compiling such inventories as a means of setting priorities for the content of ethics courses. The tentative list offered here frames the problems in terms of law making, breaking and enforcing, from the standpoint of themes running across the criminal justice system and specific situations faced by officials at each decision point in the system. It also distinguishes the problems of line decisionmakers, administrators, researchers, and teachers.

5. Which ethical theories and frameworks should be used to analyze the real-life problems of criminal justice?

There are many competing moral frameworks that can be applied to criminal justice ethics. Some of them are widely rejected, such as the theory that might makes right. But others are widely accepted, and the means for choosing among them are unclear. Mill's utilitarian framework and Rawls's deontological framework may produce very different conclusions, but teachers must be very clear about the reasoning principles on which they differ.

6. What are the best teaching methods for ethics in criminal justice, and who is most qualified to use them?

The effectiveness of different teaching methods is always hard to determine, and the process of making value judgments is harder to teach than the memorization of facts. The Hastings Center project on ethics discovered a wide range of teaching methods. With people trained in both philosophy and criminal justice teaching the course, a variety of teaching tools would seem to be advisable.

The rest of this chapter makes the case for the need to teach ethics in criminal justice, as well as the historical context of that need and the meaning of the various kinds of ethics.

B. The Case for Ethics

As the recent efforts at Harvard and other colleges have found in trying to define an "educated person," the definition must include an ability to reflect on moral questions in a mature and thorough manner. No matter whether one holds broad or narrow goals for higher education, few would deny the goal of inculcating good citizenship. As the historical context of this argument suggests, the specialization of higher education left most students without any experience in coping with moral questions and therefore left them less well prepared to be good citizens—or even to define what good citizenship is.

This case is made more fully and more persuasively elsewhere (Hastings Center, 1980:7–8). My primary argument is that the teaching of ethics may be even more important in criminology and criminal justice curriculums for two general reasons: the nature of the subject matter; and the nature of the vocations many students of this subject matter ultimately pursue.

1. Nature of the Subject

The study of rulemaking, breaking and enforcing,* is first and foremost the study of moral behavior. To study it empirically and scientifically—to document, explain, and predict the observed

*I will leave the definitions of, and differences between, criminology and criminal justice to those more concerned with semantics and professional labels.

patterns of variation in that behavior—is important, but that is not the only perspective that can or should be brought to bear on it. If students are to spend many days of their lives learning the correlates of juvenile delinquency, homosexuality, the history of the law of theft, or the effectiveness of police strategies to reduce robberies, they should have more than just a commonsense understanding of why these issues are important.

The deviance school of criminology, especially in England, criticized traditional criminologists for taking it for granted that all laws were right, all crime was bad, and that crime and its responses should be studied sui generis rather than as part of the broader social processes of deviating from nonlegal norms, rules, and conventions (Walton, Taylor, and Young, 1973). The solution, at least for those who did not embrace a Marxist approach to criminology, was to abandon value judgments about any kind of moral behavior and study it all without a view to correcting or changing it (see Reiman, 1979, for a philosophical defense of that approach). But as citizens, we are all forced to make value judgments about moral behavior, and scholarly inquiry is needed to help us all make those judgments.

A different solution to the problem of taking the law for granted, then, is to examine the law, crime, and enforcement critically from an ethical, and not just a scientific, standpoint. Scientific criminologists have already looked at moral behavior empirically with a critical stance, showing whose interests are served by various laws (see, for example, Gusfield's [1966] study of Prohibition). But they have not gone on to consider whether it is just or good for the law to serve those interests. Laws against theft clearly serve the rich more than the poor, but it is hard to find a current ethical theory that would justify burglary, robbery, or fraud. Criminology need not fear being "correctionalist" (Matza, 1969) in its goals (as opposed to its methods) as long as it has an adequate ethical analysis concluding that the behavior to be corrected is immoral.*

*A hyperscientistic graduate student once accused a professor of criminal justice of being unethical as a scientist for espousing this view. I suspect the taxpayers who paid the professors' salaries did not mind their university criminologists taking an interest in reducing crime, although there should also be a place for pure theoreticians who are totally disinterested in the question.

The addition of moral philosophy to our current exclusively scientific or sometimes technical, "how-to-do-it" approach to criminology would provide both scholarship and teaching with a more complete and richer understanding of the nature of the subject matter.

Not that both the philosophy and the science need to be done by the same scholars. There may even be good reasons, in the proper scientific "appreciation" or observation of crime, for those who use science to study crime to avoid explicit considerations of ethical questions about what they study. But as Gouldner (1962) has argued, social scientists already have values and cannot help dealing with the ethics of what they study, at least implicitly. Surely those criminologists who gave explicit consideration to the ethics of the behavior they study scientifically cannot be said, a priori, to be any less scientific as a result.

No matter what personnel arrangements are made for research and teaching, the subject matter of criminology will be incompletely taught unless ethics is brought into the curriculum. A student of crime who has not thought about whether and when violence is right or wrong can hardly be said to have a thorough understanding of the subject.

Moreover, the nature of the subject matter makes it almost impossible for ethics to be ignored in teaching. Since teachers are already introducing their value judgments implicitly, the explicit teaching of ethics may be merely a change in approach rather than scope. It would also help teachers to recognize their own value systems; even those who take a neutral stance toward current laws and their enforcement are taking a value position—the position that the status quo is not clearly unjust.

2. Nature of Students' Vocations

Just as the study of criminology and criminal justice is the study of morality, those whose vocations lead them to the criminal justice system will confront constant moral decisions throughout their work life. These decisions are uniquely important. Two factors distinguish the moral decisions of criminal justice agents from those of business people, engineers, and doctors. First, criminal justice decisions are made on behalf of society as a whole, a collective moral judgment made in trust, usually by a single person. That would seem to entail a far greater responsibility than is assigned to other vocations. Second, the decisions criminal justice agents make are not just incidentally, but are primarily, moral decisions. An engineer designs a building that may or may not kill people, but the decision is primarily a technical one and only incidentally a moral one. When a police officer decides to arrest someone who has disturbed a neighborhood late at night, and when a judge decides to let that person out on a suspended sentence, the decisions are primarily moral ones (Is it right to punish this person?) and only incidentally technical ones.

All those who wield power in any setting must come to grips with what William Ker Muir, Jr. (1977) calls "the morality of coercion," the use of harm against some people to prevent even greater harm against themselves or others. Parents punish children, managers fire incompetent employees, professors fail students who do not turn in papers. But agents of the criminal justice system use far greater coercion than any other professional. Doctors and engineers may make decisions determining the life or death of many people, but only a criminal justice agent is expected to cause intentionally the death of healthy members of society on behalf of that society, or to deprive people of their liberty for extended periods of time. Philosophical analyses of the morality of coercion may (or may not) vary little in the abstract from punishing children to capital punishment, but the emotional impact of the decision to punish (or not) on those who must do it is probably greater when the punishment is more severe.

Not all students in criminology and criminal justice programs will end up in positions requiring them to make decisions about severe coercion. Many will never be employed in criminal justice, whereas others will only hold staff jobs well removed from the business of making moral judgments about and coercing citizens. Even big-city police officers on patrol will only fire their guns at other people, on average, once every ten to twenty years (Sherman and Blumberg, 1981). But as long as criminology and criminal justice programs remain the central academic preparation for criminal justice agents (Sherman, et al., 1978), we are obliged as educators to prepare our students for the moral dilemmas of criminal justice. Indeed, the case could be made that all citizens should have a working knowledge of the ethical problems in criminal justice, simply to make them intelligent voters and to help them fulfill civic responsibilities.

The need for ethics can easily be written off as an impractical proposal at a time in which the entire future of crime-related teaching is in doubt. Sharp enrollment declines have been reported in several well-known programs, and more declines can be expected with the apparently certain end of federal Law Enforcement Assistance Administration (LEAA) "block grants" for state and local criminal justice activities. The end of that funding will put thousands of graduates of criminology and criminal justice programs out of work. Combined with the cutbacks in police and other criminal justice employment in many parts of the country, the LEAA cuts will make criminal justice even less attractive as a vocation, possibly depressing enrollments even more than would be predicted from the declining numbers of people of the traditional college-going age. Finally, the lack of new funds for the federal Law Enforcement Education Program (LEEP), which once supported almost 90,000 students with $40 million a year, may cause even more financial difficulties for crime-related higher education.

These practical problems suggest several reasons not to introduce ethics to the curriculum. A faculty without a moral philosopher may not be able to hire one under these conditions, and borrowing a professor from the philosophy department will only help philosophy's financial situation at the expense of criminology or criminal justice. Existing scientific or practitioner faculty cannot be spared to be trained in moral philosophy. Teaching materials are insufficient to satisfy the students. Students may refuse to major in the program if ethics is required, and may only ignore it if it is elective.

Some or all of these objections may be true. Some of them might be overcome. None of them is morally compelling in relation to the need for ethics teaching. That is, while these may be difficult practical problems, none of them is a persuasive ethical justification for not teaching ethics. Even so, this study will address these and other practical problems to make it as easy as possible to fit ethics into the curriculum.

C. The Historical Context

Given the need for ethics in the very nature of the subject matter and students' vocations in criminal justice, it may be surprising that the field has developed without explicit attention to ethics. But given the historical context of ethics teaching in higher education, it is easier to understand.

The past century has witnessed the fall and rise of moral philosophy in the American college curriculum. Douglas Sloan (1980:2) has described the lofty place ethics once held: "Throughout most of the 19th century the most important course in the college curriculum was moral philosophy, taught usually by the college president, and required of all senior students. The moral philosophy course was regarded as the capstone of the curriculum. It aimed to pull together, to integrate, and to give meaning and purpose to the students' entire college experience and course of study. In so doing, it even more importantly sought to equip the graduating seniors with the ethical sensitivity and insight needed in order to put their newly acquired knowledge to use in ways that would benefit not only themselves and their own personal advancement, but the larger society as well." These courses conveyed a sense of shared values, and apparently reflected a strongly affirmative view on Socrates' question of whether virtue can be taught. That is, in the predominantly religious colleges of the day, the teaching of moral philosophy appeared to have been a vehicle for the teaching of morals.

The fall of moral philosophy from its central place in the curriculum has been traced to several factors (Rosen and Caplan, 1980; Hastings Center, 1980). Perhaps the master trend was the specialization and compartmentalization of the curriculum, spurred by the rise of science and social science, which made it impossible to unify the curriculum around any single subject or perspective. And just as scientists began to write for their colleagues and not for the lay public, philosophers shifted from addressing issues of general public interest to more difficult and complex questions of metaethics, which "came to constitute the mainstream of English language ethics well into the 1960s. Rather than being thought of as 'soft,' philosophy—as if to ape science—became one of the 'hardest' and most specialized disciplines," (Rosen and Caplan, 1980:3). The "hardness" no doubt helped to scare away many potential students, save in those few colleges where general education or distribution requirements forced them to take an ethics course.

The social and academic changes of the 1970s brought at least some teaching of ethics out of the philosophy departments, out of metaethics, away from theoretical questions, and toward more applied questions. The new ethic courses are now placed nearer to (if not central to) the major public issues of the day. The full reasons for this trend are far from clear, but there are at least three likely candidates. First, the Watergate, corporate bribery, and government intelligence scandals reminded us that many public and private leaders behave immorally in their work, with harmful results for the society. Second, the increase in malpractice litigation against doctors, engineers, teachers, and other professionals put the "ethics" (or morality) of those groups under the public spotlight as well. Third, the major shift of undergraduate enrollments (Carnegie Foundation, 1977:103) into professional and preprofessional courses spurred many educators into finding ways to fuse the liberal arts into curriculums focused on specific careers. Thus, The Hastings Center Report (1980:22) found that an increasing number of courses and programs in ethics are aimed at preprofessional students. Finally, there is a growing concern within professions themselves, changes prompted by changing technologies, economics, and other forces separate from external attacks.

Given the diverse forces contributing to the rise of ethics courses, it is not surprising that The Hastings Center (1980:22) also found that the pressure to begin new ethics courses has come from many sources, including students, faculty, administrators, and professional societies. What is surprising is that few of those sources appear to have done the same for criminology or criminal justice programs. While I have no recent survey of courses to document this impression, the research done for the National Advisory Commission on Higher Education for police officers in 1976–78 found no evidence of explicit teaching of ethics in those programs. Yet during the same period, applied and professional ethics courses in other fields were growing rapidly.

Consider the contrast. Virtually every medical school and 80 percent of the nursing schools offered at least some introduction to ethics by the mid-1970s (Clouser, 1980:45–46). The 64 percent of law schools *offering* legal ethics courses in 1958 grew to 85 percent that required such courses (in compliance with ABA requirements) by 1978, as well as an increase in teachers specializing in legal ethics and more scholarship on those issues (Kelly, 1980). Other fields are less impressive, but they still show substantial activity in ethics. Twenty-seven percent of journalism schools teach a specific course on professional ethics (Christians and Covert, 1980:11). Eighty percent of graduate business schools responding to a 1978 survey reported offering special courses in "public policy," which generally includes business ethics (Powers and Vogel, 1980:31). Almost 20 percent of the programs in public policy and public administration responding to a 1978 survey required a course in ethics (Fleishman and Payne, 1980:57).

Criminology and criminal justice curriculums are not alone, however, in their apparent disregard of ethical issues. Less than 10 percent of the engineering schools surveyed in 1975 taught "professionalism" (including ethics) as a separate course (Baum, 1980:22). And in the social sciences generally (including some criminology and criminal justice programs) only about fifteen courses on ethical issues are taught in the entire country (Warwick, 1980:2).

Nor is the state of ethics teaching in professional education programs all that it could be. Many of the programs are hampered by the lack of solid scholarly material, by a strong sense on the part of many faculty members of inadequate preparation to teach courses in ethics, and by the difficulty of getting students to take ethics courses as seriously as the more vocation-oriented courses. (Hastings Center, 1980:26). Many of them seem to raise *moral* issues without venturing on into *ethical* analysis. In business courses, for example, "ethics regularly pop up as an issue of appropriate concern, but almost never as a method of analysis" (Powers and Vogel, 1980:31).

Overall, the current state of ethics teaching in higher education is clearly a mixed picture. If it is better off than its relative obscurity for most of the century, it is still nowhere near widespread acceptance. The conclusions of The Hastings Center Report (1980:5-6) are instructive: "Probably the majority of professional schools still offer nothing of a serious and systematic nature in ethics, and hundreds of undergraduate institutions—most of which stress the importance of ethics in the introductions to their catalogues—offer little in the way of ethics other than some traditional (and usually elective) departmental offerings in philosophy and religion. . . . At some schools there is considerable enthusiasm, while at others there is indifference or outright rejection." In general, The Hastings Center (1980:2) found, "great enthusiasm is bewilderingly counterpoised against an equally great lack of interest."

There are a few recent signs of interest in ethics in criminology and criminal justice. Under a grant from the National Endowment for the Humanities, Professor Michael Feldberg at Boston University has held several summer workshops on teaching ethics and other humanities in police academies and community college programs. The instructors participating in the workshop have returned to their institutions to fit in the humanistic perspective, although more often in the context of existing courses rather than through a creation of separate courses.

More recently, a curriculum subcommittee of the John Jay College of Criminal Justice in New York, simultaneously the nation's largest criminal justice program and a college offering majors in other fields, recommended that all John Jay students should be required to take a one-term course in introductory ethics (Strickland, 1980). John Jay's government and public administration majors are alrady required to take an ethics course from the college's philosophy department. The committee recommended that the "Introduction to Ethics" course be described as follows:

> Do objective moral standards exist or is morality relative to culture or individuals? This course examines the principles that guide moral reasoning and argumentation. The main theories of ethical justification are analyzed, with application to such selected issues of social morality as punishment, civil disobedience, privacy and sexual behavior, war, racial and sexual equality, abortion, euthanasia, business integrity, and economic justice (Strickland, 1980).

Other scattered signs of interest in ethics teaching may be found elsewhere in criminology and criminal justice. American University, for example, has required a course on the ethics of criminal justice, and offered advanced courses for the past decade. With two trained philosophers on the faculty of the School of Justice, American University probably has done more than most other universities to encourage this interest.

Lack of interest however, is probably far greater. It may be safe to say that even where ethics is taught, it is only marginal to the curriculum (as at Albany, where there is almost no link between ethics per se and any of the comprehensive doctoral examinations, the central focus of the curriculum). In most institutions, separate courses on criminal justice ethics are probably unknown, and the teaching of ethics in other courses is unlikely to be explicit in its use of formal philosophical tools.

Nonetheless, criminal justice curricula appear to be in a state of transition. In a period of seeking new directions (or attempting to survive), it may be that anything goes. Precisely because of the problems faced by criminal justice education, this may be one of the most favorable times to attempt to bring ethics into the curriculum. But before doing so, it is helpful to be clear about what kind of ethics should be taught.

D. Defining Terms

There is a good deal of colloquial confusion, on the one hand, about words describing the actual judgments and rules that are made about what is right and wrong, good and bad, obligatory or not, and on the other hand, the study or analysis of those judgments and rules. Some people define the judgments as *morals,* and the process of reasoning and analysis underlying or criticizing morals as *ethics*. Given that distinction, the subject here can be defined as teaching the study and reasoning related to morals, and not the teaching of morality (Frankena, 1973:4; Hastings Center, 1980:13). Ethics is, then, the philosophy of morals and not a set of rules—as the commonplace "code of ethics" erroneously implies. Under this definition, the codes should be known as "codes of morals," or "rules of conduct," for it is doubtful that their authors meant to establish a code for the study of moral questions.

While some would take issue with this definition of ethics, there is more agreement about the different branches of ethics: descriptive ethics, metaethics, and normative ethics. *Descriptive ethics* is the empirical study of human morals and behavior by any discipline that addresses the question of how people *do* behave. Descriptive ethics is not concerned with how people *should* behave. Although philosophers use it as a category to distinguish it from other branches of ethics, descriptive ethics clearly embraces the whole of criminology as Sellin (1938) defined it: the description and explanation of rule-making, rule-breaking, and rule-enforcing.

Metaethics is the study of the concepts and terms that underlie reasoning about morals. It considers questions such as "What is justice?" "Can value judgments or morals be justified at all?" "What is the difference between the moral and the nonmoral?" While many philosophers are concerned with metaethical questions for their own sakes, answering these questions also contributes to resolving actual moral questions.

Normative ethics is the study of moral questions, or the provision of reasons for decisions about what is right or wrong and what ought to be done in particular situations. It is also concerned with those traits of character (in contrast to specific decisions and actions) that are worthy of praise or blame and of the kinds of institutions and societies that are just or unjust. Duties and obligations, rights and responsibilities, virtues and vices: the identification of these concepts in real life are all the territory of normative ethics.

A newer category of ethics, *"applied ethics,"* might be called a distinctive approach to normative ethics, rather than a subcategory of it. More sharply focused on making actual choices in moral conflicts than is normative ethics in general, "it draws on ethical theory, on moral principles, on the study of methods of choice to reach or to scrutinize moral judgments" (Hastings Center, 1980:15). Applied ethics studies questions of both personal choice, such as whether someone should have an abortion; and collective, institutional, or social choice, such as whether abortions should be subsidized by the state.

A more traditional category, *professional ethics,* is clearly part of applied ethics. Professional ethics is the philosophical study of both personal and collective moral choices about conduct and problems arising in work settings. While the occupations claiming the mantle of "profession" have a longer tradition of examining these questions, the term has been used to describe all work-related applied ethics (Hastings Center, 1980:15).

Here the term "ethics" is used as shorthand for normative ethics. Its primary concern is with applied, professional ethics, as the section on the scope of ethical problems in criminology and criminal justice makes clear.

II. The Aims of Ethics

Even among those who accept the need for the teaching of ethics, there is much debate over what the specific goals of that teaching should be. At the height of the Watergate scandal, the news media gave considerable attention to the fact that one of the convicted presidential aides had, during his college years, studied ethics with the Reverend William Sloane Coffin, Jr., then the chaplain of Yale University. The implication was that Coffin had failed as a teacher because the Nixon aide had admittedly offended against law and morals in order to secure his position in the White House. What good is ethics teaching if it cannot make people be moral?

Most ethics educators reject the goal of making people moral as naive and unrealistic. The forces shaping individual behavior, as criminologists well know, are multiple and complex and are not likely to be substantially altered by a one-semester course on how to think about moral problems. The goals I would suggest are less ambitious but no less important, for they may still affect the kind of person the college graduate becomes. Five of them are taken from The Hastings Center Report (1980:47-52), which applies to all teaching of ethics in higher education. The other three goals are more specifically tailored to teaching ethics in criminology and criminal justice.

The Hastings Center Report concluded that "the primary purpose of courses in ethics ought to be to provide students with those concepts and analytical skills that will enable them to grapple with broad ethical theory in attempting to resolve both personal and professional dilemmas, as well as to reflect on the moral issues facing the larger society." It elaborated on this purpose with five specific goals:

A. Stimulating the Moral Imagination

At its best, ethics takes moral judgment beyond emotions and into careful cognitive reasoning. But emotional sensitivity to ethical issues is needed to supply the energy for cognitive reasoning. As Fleishman and Payne (1980:11) put it, this goal is to raise the "level of moral anxiety." Stimulating materials, such as novels, movies, and students' personal experiences, can often be more effective in arousing emotions over ethical issues than standard philosophical texts. But the goal must be to direct emotional energy toward cognitive efforts: discovering contradictions in one's own moral views, understanding how other people's moral reasoning affects their lives, seeing the hidden assumptions that seem to lead to immoral conclusions. Most important, it should be channeled to learning that an initial emotional reaction to an issue may not be what one later concludes, and that more reflective judgments may be more often correct.

B. Recognizing Ethical Issues

Minneapolis Police Chief Anthony V. Bouza (1977) has argued that police administrators generally ask only how to get things done, not whether it is right to do them. Certainly it is easier to go through life without raising ethical questions concerning widespread social practices. The recognition of ethical issues in war, the distribution and allocation of food, and even the population implications of motherhood over the past fifteen years has been the source of major social conflicts, and many public officials may wish that there was less recognition of ethical issues. Once students' moral imaginations have been stimulated, however, they should be given opportunities to recognize moral issues in technical problems that they would not have considered before. As the technology and social relations of our society keep changing, this skill will become even more important in the future.

C. Developing Analytical Skills

The tools of ethical analysis are concepts, principles, and prescriptive moral judgments. Concepts such as "justice," "liberty," and "good"; principles such as "act as to treat humanity . . . in every case as an end and never merely as a means"; and moral judgments such as "capital punishment is wrong" are all central to moral reasoning. So are the ethical theories and frameworks for analysis that various philosophers have developed over the centuries, some of which have been widely rejected, but some of which have been kept in use. All of these tools, if used properly, help to force a student to maintain coherence and consistency of thought. Some of the ethical frameworks have their own inconsistencies, but they are far more coherent than most colloquial treatments of ethical issues. Without these tools and a solid grasp of their proper use, ethical reasoning is unlikely to pass beyond the level of dormitory or locker-room bull sessions.

D. Eliciting a Sense of Moral Obligation and Personal Responsibility

This goal consists of showing a student why he or she ought to be moral and showing what it means to take ethics seriously. The concept of personal responsibility is a foundation for this discourse, because individuals must be presumed to have the freedom to make moral choices if they are to take ethics seriously.

E. Tolerating—and Resisting—Disagreement and Ambiguity

This goal recognizes that disagreements will always occur, and that most moral issues are ambiguous rather than clear-cut. Students should be encouraged to understand and respect the disagreements, especially in a society that has made a collective moral judgment in favor of freedom of speech and thought. At the same time, they should learn to resist it, since it *is* possible for ethical issues to be solved, and they must learn to come to decisions on their own. Indeed, one aspect of this goal is that students be able to dispense with the need for a teacher in order to handle moral issues.

In addition to these general goals suggested by The Hastings Center Report, I would suggest three other specific goals for crime-related higher education:

F. Understanding the Morality of Coercion

The business of criminal justice is forcing people to do what they do not want to do, on pain of physical harm or death. Some people never appreciate the full moral and social consequences of that task until after they have become criminal justice agents, and the result can be a substantial "reality shock" (Westley, 1970). Muir (1977) has suggested that the ability to understand and accept coercion as tragically necessary and moral can make a substantial difference in how well police officers perform their jobs. It is not clear, again, whether a one-semester course can change what may be a basic personality trait—the moral attitude toward the use of coercion—but this goal may at least help people make better choices about their vocations. Whether or not one actually exercises coercion, this goal is also important for the study of crime and punishment. The criminal justice agent only makes decisions within the range of discretion that our society allows. All of us share the responsibility for setting that range of discretion.

G. Integrating Technical and Moral Competence

For those students who do go on to action, teaching, or research in criminal justice or criminology, the teaching of ethics should help them form the habit of considering moral and technical issues simultaneously.

The police officer should be able to use deadly force both accurately and morally, quickly processing the information about a given situation in terms of moral principles that he or she has already thought about. The judge should be technically competent to predict the consequences of a sentence for both the defendant and the community. At the same time, the judge should be morally competent to consider the equity of the sentence in relation to sentences the judge has given to like offenders for like offenses. The researcher should be able to consider simultaneously the methodological strength of a random assignment, experimental research design, and the moral implications of systematically giving some people and not others what may be a benefit or a harm.

H. Becoming Familiar with the Full Range of Moral Issues Specific to Criminology and Criminal Justice

Previous goals included teaching students to recognize ethical issues and to be able to dispense with the teacher. Both of those goals could make this one superfluous, assuming they were always fully realized. Since uniform success is unlikely, however, this goal provides additional insurance that students will both recognize the issues and understand the moral arguments surrounding present practices in criminal justice and criminological research. As Section IV shows, there is a wide range of ethical issues in criminal justice, from affirmative action to lying, that require thoughtful reflection by those who confront them. As long as higher education programs are already specifically focused on the problems of criminal justice, the ethical dimensions of those problems should be given equal (if not greater) weight to their technical aspects.

These eight goals could be labeled as substantive in nature, concerned with the outcome of the teaching process: how students will be different as a result of the teaching. The goals are distinct from procedural goals, the means to achieve the substantive goals: how the teaching should be done. I raise this point only because there are three procedural goals widely used under the rubric of ethics (Hastings Center, 1980:12) that are *not* appropriate for the substantive goals I have described. These procedures, or approaches, are known as values clarification, values inquiry and analysis, and moral development.

Values clarification is a movement found in both academic and nonacademic settings that tries to foster personal growth through increased self-awareness (Simon, Howe and Kirschenbaum, 1972). Its method is to help people identify and specify their personal values and to find a way of rank-ordering those values. The focus of the approach seems to be on the self, rather than on moral decisions.

Values inquiry and analysis is a method of understanding human situations through the values that motivate human choice and decision. It is a method of interpreting human behavior rather than a tool for either personal growth or distinguishing right from wrong.

Moral development attempts to use education as a means of encouraging natural growth through the patterned stages of cognitive moral reasoning hypothesized by Jean Piaget and Lawrence Kohlberg. Kohlberg (1976), for example, posits six stages of moral reasoning from simple obedience to rules in the face of a threat of punishment, to an orientation to being seen as a "good boy or girl," to a contractual, legalistic orientation, to the highest and most mature stage of moral reasoning: the orientation to conscience or principle. Since each student can be classified according to his or her stage of moral development through standardized tests, courses are often taught and evaluated with the explicit goal of raising the student's developmental stage. There is some empirical evidence that active participation in moral discussion, guided by a skilled teacher, does increase the measured moral development stage.

None of these approaches, or procedural goals, is appropriate for the substantive goals suggested earlier, since none of them show how to answer what Frankena (1973:12) calls "the primary question" of normative ethics: "How may or should we decide or determine what is morally right for a certain agent (oneself or another, possibly a group or a whole society) to do, or what he morally ought to do, in a certain situation?" The procedural goal for normative ethics is simply to have students understand and deal with that kind of question in as rational and coherent a manner as possible.

III. Fitting Ethics in

If we grant both the need for ethics and the specific aims of ethics teaching, how can and should ethics be fit into the existing curricula in criminology and criminal justice? Assuming that it should be done well, if it is to be done at all, the way to fit ethics in will depend on the criteria one establishes for doing it well. Three criteria come to mind.

A. Criteria for Fitting Ethics in

The first criterion is that ethics should be fit in so that it is accorded *serious treatment* in the curriculum. There is a widespread fear among faculty members that ethics courses outside of departments of philosophy and religion are "part of a broad trend toward the softening or evasion of academic standards" (Hastings Center, 1980:76–77). And in law schools, as one example, a 1975–76 school year survey of 1,300 law students found that they see their required ethics courses as being weak: " . . . the ethics course in law schools has low esteem in the curriculum hierarchy; it is perceived by students to be less valuable, to require less time and effort, and to be worse taught in comparison to most other law school courses" (Kelly, 1980:2–3, reporting on Pipkin, 1979). Ironically, a 1977 survey of legal ethics teachers (also reported in Kelly) found no concern about student attitudes toward the ethics courses, which underlines the danger of ethics courses becoming "guts" without the faculty concerned knowing it. The result may be not just a failure to accomplish the goals of ethics teaching, but as Pipkin concluded from his law student survey, it may even convey the message that ethics is unimportant. If the institution teaching it doesn't take it seriously, why should the students?

The second criterion is that ethics in criminal justice should be *taught explicitly as ethics*, and not as law, public policy, or some other approach to making value judgments. Constitutional arguments are, in one sense, debates within the ethical framework of the Constitution and prior Supreme Court cases. Public policy analysis is premised on some conception of the public good, implicitly using some ethical scheme (such as rule-utilitarianism) as well as extensive factual analysis to arrive at conclusions. Many moral issues in criminal justice are currently taught with one or both of these perspectives. But both depend on moral philosophy, and both are essentially modified or boiled-down versions of ethical argument. Students will understand both perspectives better by understanding the philosophical foundations on which they are built. They will also have a clearer picture of the role of ethics when they discover that legal and ethical analysis can lead to different and contradictory results. Capital punishment, for example, can be both constitutional (according to the Supreme Court) and unethical (according to one possible Rawlsian analysis).

It follows that the third criterion must be the *competent teaching* of ethics by those who are trained (or have trained themselves well) in moral philosophy. Unless the instructor (or at least one partner in a team-teaching effort) is well grounded in the various frameworks of moral philosophy—as well as knowledgeable about the concrete problems of criminal justice—then the ethics teaching can be neither serious nor explicit. The lack of competent teaching, for example, may explain the low esteem in which law students hold their ethics courses. Kelly (1980:27), noting that most legal ethics teachers have less than two years teaching experience in the area, suggests that "the course, like the queen of spades, may be passed around among the faculty with some degree of regularity, and could be construed as some support for Pipkin's (1979) conclusion that, at least at a number of schools, the course is poorly taught," It is unlikely that teachers newly assigned to teach an ethics course in any professional field will be well enough grounded in moral philosophy to teach ethical issues and frameworks explicitly, thus bringing an unfortunately loose and "soft" approach to the teaching. Again, the result may be no better than dormitory bull sessions.

B. Two Models: Pervasive or Separate

The three criteria can be used to make several choices about how to fit ethics into the curriculum. The most obvious and basic choice is whether to teach ethics in a separate course designed for that purpose, or to weave it into all aspects and courses of the curriculum. The latter approach has been described as the "pervasive" model of teaching ethics. There are merits to both approaches, especially in criminology and criminal justice. Ethical issues can be identified in almost any subject or course, but no explicit grounding in ethical tools is usually offered.

The major problem with the pervasive method is that in the collegial governance system of a faculty it is more difficult to train and require each professor to consider ethics in his or her courses than it is to have one professor specialize in ethics. The training is especially important, for assuming that every professor handles ethical questions competently is equal to assuming that there are no special skills or tools of ethical analysis to be learned or taught. At best, the pervasive method can raise ethics as a concern, but it is doubtful that it can use ethics effectively in a wide range of courses. Time alone would not permit the introduction of the tools of ethical analysis, in addition to covering the material from both scientific and ethical perspectives.

Moreover, consider the argument in The Hastings Center (1980:75) Report against the pervasive model: "The training of most professionals gives them no systematic background in ethics, much less enough of a background to allow them to handle ethical issues as competently as they handle issues in their own professional field. There is no reason to expect that most professors would care to give a significant segment of their courses to the ethical problems of their disciplines. Most have heavy enough responsibilities as it is. With the 'pervasive method,' students do not bring up many issues, and actually devote little time to discussing those that do come up. *Perhaps most important, the diffusion of ad hoc ethical analysis among a wide variety of courses deprives students of the opportunity to focus systematically on ethical problems for their own sake*, and also of a context for giving them a coherent means of developing broader views on the nature of ethics. For all these reasons, we think students should have at least one well-organized, reasonably long course in ethics at both the undergraduate and the professional school level." [Emphasis added].

On the other hand, merely offering a separate course on ethics, especially if it is not well taught or not taught by a respected teacher, might foster the view of the role of ethics as marginal in the curriculum. Just as staff units in planning and crime analysis in police agencies have encouraged precinct captains to think they had no responsibility to plan or analyze, a separate course in ethics might reinforce the current rigid separation of ethical and scientific questions. And in the more prestigious departments, there is no question that the separation is highly unequal in favor of science. If ethics were given an important role through the pervasive method in the major courses of the curriculum (such as introduction to criminal justice), then it is more likely to be accorded serious treatment.

To summarize: the pervasive method is more likely to afford ethics serious treatment but less likely to do so explicitly and competently; the separate course could be explicitly and competently taught but with an unknown risk of not being taken seriously. Under the current conditions in most criminology and criminal justice programs, it seems surer and safer to use the separate course as the starting point. If the pervasive approach can be developed—a fearsome challenge for any academic administrator—then all the better. The separate course would provide a foundation for the pervasive approach, sparing other courses the need for grounding students in analytical tools—still assuming, of course, that the faculty in other courses have a strong grasp of the tools themselves. That would take a long time to accomplish even with their full cooperation, which seems unlikely.

In those departments or programs in which separate courses cannot be or are not implemented, the pervasive model *might* be better than nothing, still assuming that whatever teaching of ethics that gets done is serious, explicit, and competent. Given the three criteria, it is probably better not to teach ethics at all—explicitly or not—if it cannot be done seriously and competently.

C. Adapting Ethics to the Curriculum

The practical problems of fitting ethics in will vary according to several factors, including the type of institution the department is in, the kind of students it serves, the background and qualifications of the faculty, and the degree of external influence on the department exercised by criminal justice agencies and other external forces. The full range of problems is beyond the scope of this discussion, but one factor affecting the practical problems should be given careful consideration: the nature of the curriculum.

There are at least three undergraduate and two graduate models of the curriculum in criminology and criminal justice. At the undergraduate level, there is the interdisciplinary social science or liberal arts model, a professional model (similar to journalism schools) and a paraprofessional model found primarily in two-year associates' degree programs (Sherman et al., 1978). At the graduate level, there is the professionally oriented M.A. and the research and teaching oriented Ph.D.

1. Liberal Arts Model

The liberal arts model offers the least difficulty in fitting ethics into the curriculum. Two options are open for establishing a separate course. One is simply requiring criminology or criminal justice majors to take an introductory applied ethics course in the philosophy department, much like the one described in the John Jay College committee report quoted earlier. Another option would be to have a professor (or team) qualified in both ethics and crime studies create a new course that introduces students to both the tools of ethical analysis (perhaps including a reading of the original texts of the major ethical theorists) and the scope of ethical issues in criminology and criminal justice. As long as the course is going to apply ethical theories to practical moral problems, it might as well consider crime-related issues instead of euthanasia or abortion. The one drawback to this second option may be that there are few course materials available that integrate ethical theory with specific criminal justice issues (other than capital punishment).

2. Professional Model

This curriculum may be less flexible than the liberal arts model about the possibility of requiring a general introduction to ethics. Admittedly, John Jay College, which was once described by its vice-president as having a professional education model for at least part of its curriculum (Reppetto, 1979), may require a general ethics course, but it is the only criminal justice or criminology "program" in the country with its own philosophy department (although some departments do have their own philosophers). If the professional model undergraduate criminal justice programs were to follow the lead of the other undergraduate professional curriculums, such as journalism and business, they would have (or hire) their own faculty members to teach an ethics course expressly tailored to the problems of professional practice. Since criminal justice programs usually try to prepare people for a variety of professions within the criminal justice system, such a course should cover the full scope of ethical problems of both line or operational decisionmakers and managers, possibly excluding the issues of research and teaching. (See section IV.) Judging by The Hastings Center's publications on the experience of those other fields, however, it may be more effective to bring in someone from the philosophy department on a joint appointment.*

3. Paraprofessional Model

Ethics is a commonly required subject in both liberal arts and many professional school curricula. In the paraprofessional model, however, one is least likely to find a warm reception to a course on ethics. Ethics courses at that level are certainly not unknown; The Hastings Center Project, for example, found a course on secretarial ethics. But the time available for course work on any subject is short in a two-year curriculum, and stu-

*The problem of teaching qualifications is given further consideration in section VII.

dent interest in a separate ethics course may be lacking or even hostile if it takes away time from more technical instruction on how to do criminal justice work.

There is some debate over whether criminal justice should be taught at all in this kind of curriculum. The Police Foundation's National Advisory Commission on Higher Education for Police Officers (Sherman, et al., 1978:7) recommended that community colleges should phase out their *terminal* two-year degree programs in police education. Nonetheless, perhaps half of the total college instruction in criminal justice (and such related fields as police science and technology) occurs in the paraprofessional model curricula. For many students, it may be their only opportunity to be exposed to ethical analysis of work issues in criminal justice practice.

Weaving ethics into other courses in the curriculum may make the most sense in this curricular model. The introductory course would be a particularly good opportunity to show students the relevance of ethics to most technical aspects of criminal justice, and how to recognize ethical issues in other courses. It would be impossible to give students a thorough grounding in the tools of ethical analysis in this context, but some introduction to moral reasoning could be offered. If done well, the ethical portion of an introductory course could even stimulate more discussion of ethical issues in other courses. Only some training in ethics would be required for the professor offering the introductory course to fit ethics into the curriculum in this manner.

4. Professional Masters Curricula

Time is also short in both the one-year (the most common) and two-year versions of an M.A. or M.S. curriculum. But at the graduate level some exposure to ethics seems all the more compelling, especially since most graduate students are unlikely to have had any previous teaching in that area. A separate course, even for only two credits, would seem well worth the sacrifice of some technical course. Although a graduate faculty may be more capable of adopting the pervasive method, they are probably no more willing (perhaps less so) than undergraduate faculty. And at that level, the students can have no legitimate complaint about having to read the comprehensive materials on ethics appropriate for a special course.

The danger of students not taking ethics seriously would be lessened if it were built into some final requirement of the degree program, such as a comprehensive examination or an M.A. essay. Some medical schools, for example, require students to devote a one-month "clerkship" in medical practice to the study of a particular issue in medical ethics.

Many of these programs are focused on management rather than operations. Where that is the case it may seem more appropriate for ethics courses to focus on moral issues in management to the exclusion of operational issues. But if managers are to manage well, they should also be familiar with the moral problems their subordinates face. While the emphasis may be placed on the managerial decisions the students do or will face, it is reasonable to assume that this will also be their first and only opportunity to consider operational-level moral issues.

5. Ph.D. Programs

The greatest opportunity for using the resources of a university philosophy department lies at the Ph.D. level in criminal justice. All doctoral students could be required (or encouraged) to take an introductory normative ethics course. In addition, a faculty member in the doctoral program could offer an applied ethics course covering the full scope of action, teaching, and research issues in criminology and criminal justice. Since the nature of the course work required in these doctoral programs beyond the first year is usually quite flexible, there should be little practical difficulty with fitting in an ethics requirement.

Not that there would be total agreement. Some faculty might object that students are being diverted from their advanced courses. Administrators might object that an ethics requirement might hurt the programs's competitive edge in what is now a field with strong competition for good doctoral students. Both might find that doctoral students who have taken ethics are more interesting to work with and better-rounded scholars, and that the ethics requirement could be used as a recruiting advantage if it were presented properly. In any case, doctoral programs would have the fewest resource problems and the most flexibility in fitting in ethics.

Moreover, doctoral programs are the logical starting point for bringing ethics into the curriculum on other levels. Once faculty members have been trained in ethics in their doctoral programs, the resource difficulties with offering ethics in masters and undergraduate programs will be overcome.

D. Timing

In all these models the question of timing may be very important. The delay of ethics teaching in law schools until the third year (Kelly, 1980) seems to contribute to the lack of seriousness accorded those courses. Students are generally the most enthusiastic and openminded, if not the most sophisticated, in the first year of a program, no matter what the level. With a difficult or nontraditional course, such as ethics, it may make sense to capitalize on that freshness and enthusiasm and offer ethics during the first term of a program. One medical school even capitalizes on both freshness and sophistication by requiring a week-long introduction to medical ethics the first year, segments of other courses allocated to ethics later in the first and second years, and an intensive (but elective) seminar in the fourth year (Hastings Center, 1980:73). Criminal justice programs may need to offer different types of courses for students with and without field experience, or vary the timing to ensure that the students have all had some contact with the field. Each program may have different temporal patterns of student interest, but whatever they are, they should be considered in placing ethics in the curriculum schedule.

E. Scope of Agency Coverage

Criminology and criminal justice curricula also vary according to their substantive scope of coverage. Some are concerned primarily with police, some with corrections, some with the entire criminal justice system but not separate components of the system. The substantive scope of any ethics teaching they include might vary accordingly, but not necessarily.

Two goals might be considered in selecting the scope of an ethics course. One is the goal of familiarizing students with issues they will face, or giving them an ethical perspective on issues they already have faced. This goal implies the broadest substantive scope possible for a course, because students will have diverse backgrounds and future job experiences.

The other goal is to help contribute to raising the level of ethical discussion and practice in a professional or occupational field corresponding to a particular criminal justice agency. A course on police ethics, or ethics in corrections, can examine the ethical issues in those fields in much greater depth than a broader course on criminal justice and criminology. The instructor's research and writing that helps him or her enrich the course may be more likely to make a contribution to practice in that field. The students in any kind of course are most likely to work for only one kind of agency in any case; a course focused on their own agency might better help them to bring or apply the ethical dialogue to their work than a course that only touches lightly on their agency and then moves on to other topics.

The agency focus obviously limits the usefulness of a course to students whose work experience is or will be with other agencies. The extent of diversity in the student body might therefore be a major criterion in offering a broad or specific course. The competence of the instructor across all the issues, rather than in one area, might also be another factor; it may be better to have a strong course on police ethics than a weak course on ethics in criminal justice.

IV. Scope of Ethical Problems

Whatever agency scope a course or section of a course may adopt, the instructor may find it useful to have a fairly comprehensive inventory of ethical issues to select from. The following list is only a starting point or first attempt at such an inventory. Others should add to or reorganize it to make it more useful. The very conception of the list should change and grow as philosophical discussion of these issues develops. The list is notably weak on issues in agencies other than the police, about which I have done little reading or research, but it does provide an illustration of how an inventory might be approached. It also briefly notes the availability of teaching materials and the relative significance of each issue.

Ethical issues can be organized around a variety of dimensions. One is Thorsten Sellin's (1938) three categories in his classic definition of criminology: the study of rule-making, rule-breaking, and rule-enforcing. Another dimension is the nature and location of the moral agents making decisions, notably line officials making operating decisions about individual cases versus agency managers making policy decisions. A third approach is to classify moral decisions as either cutting across the entire criminal justice system or applying only to specific agencies or decision points. A fourth approach is to separate issues arising in the context of crime and criminal justice action, research on that action, and teaching about that action.

This inventory combines several of the dimensions, concentrating on the action issues in the law-enforcing category (including the full range of the criminal justice system), with brief consideration of research and teaching issues.

A. Action Issues

1. Lawmaking

The question of which behaviors that are banned by law ought not to be banned enjoys a rich philosophical tradition from John Stuart Mill onward. Personal pleasure in all its forms, from gambling to smoking marijuana, has been a controversial issue for legalization or prohibition for the entire history of our nation. Solid criminal justice and legal treatises, such as Packer (1968) or Morris and Hawkins (1970), provide a contemporary presentation, as do the recent presidential commission reports on obscenity, gambling, and crime.

What has received less attention are those behaviors that are not now illegal but perhaps should be because they cause harm to others. Ralph Nader's proposal to ban smoking in all public places is one example; requirements that dog owners clean up their dogs' feces left on city streets, or that nuclear energy be abandoned by public utilities as too dangerous are others. The practicality of using the criminal sanction against such behavior is often raised as an argument against proscription, but that is a separate question from whether the behavior itself is right or wrong. The broader question of what more *ought* to be proscribed is often improperly neglected. It may be far more important, at least from a utilitarian standpoint, to point out that harmful behavior (such as public smoking) is allowed than to emphasize that behavior that is nonharmful to others (such as gambling) is banned, at least when measured by the number of lives lost. The presence of "paternalistic" legislation, however annoying, may be less significant than the absence of laws needed to protect innocent persons from harm.

2. Lawbreaking

The questioning of what should be banned or allowed by law implies that some laws may be morally wrong, and that a moral person may be compelled to disobey the law—assuming that it is not more important that the law in general be obeyed, even when wrong, because of the welfare of society or benefits for the dignity of individuals. Here again, there is a rich literature on civil disobedience that can be useful as class materials: Gandhi on colonialism, Martin Luther King on segregation, and Thoreau on war are some examples. One might distinguish the violation of unjust laws as protests against the laws themselves, the violation of just laws (such as traffic regulations) in order to protest an unjust law (such as segregated bus seating), and mere law-breaking for no explicit moral purpose. The moral role of violence and revolution in unjust societies could also perhaps be examined, including the claims that some have made about the need for such violence in this country.

The metaethics of justice may be an essential part of teaching about these questions. Distinguishing just and unjust laws requires first a conception of justice, and second, of the meaning of a just law. Is a law more or less just, for example, depending on the degree to which a society supports the law? That is, is it right to argue that the broader the consensus supporting the law, the more just the law? Or is justice strictly present or absent, with degrees of justice (like pregnancy) an illogical concept? Does the sociological distinction of *mala in se* and *mala prohibita* have a valid philosophical meaning? Is it right, for example, to violate a law that is merely *mala prohibita*, but not one that is *mala in se*? What of subcultures in which social norms require certain acts, such as killing the seducer of one's daughter, forbidden by the larger society—thereby producing different definitions of *malum in se* and *prohibitum*? The central question here is whether there are objective criteria for justice, apart from what a society may believe is just.

Another issue concerning lawbreaking is the morality of the social and economic structure. If property is theft, as Proudhon (not Marx) first suggested, is it wrong for a poor person to steal from a rich person? If the law in its majestic equality forbids both the rich and the poor from sleeping under bridges and stealing bread, as Anatole France observed, is it wrong for the poor to do those things? Anyone whose work is connected with punishing poor people, which comprises the bulk of criminal justice, should at least consider these issues and not accept the law's position unreflectively.

3. Law Enforcing

a. *Line decisions across the system.* A number of moral decisions are faced by line officials in every realm of the criminal justice system. Although the constraints on those decisions vary according to both the officials' particular tasks and each specific situation, there are still some general principles of the conditions governing those decisions. At least six categories of decisions arise repeatedly in any discussion of criminal justice processing: discretion, force, due process, time, rewards, and loyalty. Many more could probably be identified.

Discretion. Law enforcement officials—from police officers to judges to parole officers—are continually faced with the questions of how to use their discretion to invoke the sanctions in their power. Arrest, charging, bail, sentencing, revocation of parole, and other decisions are all highly discretionary, as the past two decades of observational research have shown, largely because the law is *under*enforced. If every act that was vulnerable to sanction was subjected to the maximum penalty each official could invoke, then there would be no discretion about which to raise moral questions. But since suspects are not arrested despite adequate evidence, since many arrestees are not charged, since most charges are reduced, and so on, several ethical questions pervade all sanctioning decisions.

One question is whether officials are making *equitable* decisions: whether different kinds of people committing the same acts—and perhaps with the same prior criminal record—are receiving the same sanctioning decisions. Those decisions include the invoking of a sanction at all, the severity of the sanction invoked, and perhaps even the principles used to invoke the sanction. The unfettered and largely unreviewed discretion of many criminal justice officials creates a great danger of arbitrary decisionmaking affected by such irrelevant factors as mood or indigestion, not to mention racial prejudice. Observation research has consistently shown the degree of deference the suspect or "client" shows to an official to affect the decision to invoke a sanction. Whether bowing and scraping is an appropriate criterion for not arresting someone who would be arrested if he or she was rude and impolite may not be a difficult moral question, but it is a common decision (see Sherman, 1980a).

Another ethical question for discretion is the choice between risking a *false positive* or a *false negative*. In deciding to frisk someone who makes a police officer suspect that crime may be afoot, the officer risks a false positive: that the suspect may be completely innocent and not carrying any weapons. The frisked citizen may see the police action as unjust harassment and form a poor opinion of the police. But if the officer decides not to frisk a suspect, he risks a false negative: the suspect may commit an armed robbery as soon as the officer leaves, or perhaps even shoot and kill the officer. Judges making bail decisions try to predict who will and will not flee; parole boards making release decisions try to predict who will and will not commit another crime while on parole; and others face similar problems. The classic example is juries, which wrestle with the moral principle of letting ninety-nine guilty men go free in order that one innocent man may not be convicted. The criminal justice system certainly does not operate on that principle, and Supreme Court Justice William Rehnquist has even suggested that the system should not operate on the presumption of innocence (*Bell v. Wolfish*, 99 S. Ct. 1861 [1979]). The question of what principles should govern the false negative/false positive problem certainly needs careful consideration.

Still another moral question about discretion is *how* to determine which set of operational standards to use, both for maintaining equity and for dealing with the false negative/false positive problem. A judge may be perfectly consistent in all his or her decisions, but substantially more (or less) severe than most other judges in the same court. The other judges, however, may be inconsistent as individuals; the one judge who is off the norm may be the only consistent one on the bench. Who, then, is right and who is wrong? The same questions, again, can be raised about police making arrests or prison wardens making disciplinary decisions.

Force. The use of physical coercion against other people underlies all the sanctions about which the officials exercise discretion. Force is the essence of criminal justice, just as the monopoly on the legitimate use of force is the essence of the nation-state (Weber, 1964:154). The decisions of whether to use force, how much to use, and under what conditions are confronted by police officers, juries, judges, prison officials, probation and parole officers, and others. All of them face the paradox, noted earlier, of using harm to prevent harm. There is recent and rich philosophical literature on the question of capital punishment, as well as an older penological literature on how much cruelty to use in punishing criminals generally. (It is only two centuries since torture, maiming, and capital punishment for nonviolent offenses such as burglary have been widely defined officially as immoral in Western societies, partly as a result of the penological literature.) These questions, however, only cover a small portion of the scope of decisions to use force. One of the leading national issues in race relations, for example, is when police should use deadly force. It has been virtually ignored by philosophers (but see Elliston, 1979), although there is a substantial legal literature available on the question (Sherman, 1980b). The related question of whether it is immoral not to use the full force allowed by law to accomplish some purpose, such as killing a fleeing felony suspect who cannot otherwise be apprehended, also deserves far more attention.

Even more complex are the questions about using less than deadly force: when is it right to hit someone with a club, spray them with mace, or handcuff them? What kind of deliberation should be required whenever the opportunity or need to use force arises? Should there be (or can there be) any opportunities for appeal, defense on factual grounds, or other processes of decision before force is used? What sort of policies and practices should be followed to avoid *creating* many of the opportunities or necessary occasions for using force (Reiss, 1980)? What principles of a balance of risk of harm between officials, suspects, and the public should govern these decisions?

The most basic question of all criminal justice ethics, of course, is whether and under what conditions one can reconcile doing harm to others with our widespread norms against harm. The literature on pacifism and conscientious objection to war seems most relevant here, but I am not aware that any of it has been applied to the domestic use of force to maintain order. Can a pacifist be a police officer or a judge? Can a Christian? Can a Rawlsian? What is the ethical defense for saying that killing is wrong and then urging killing in response to killing? Muir (1977) has provided an insightful account of how police officers live with and adapt to such questions (some doing it well, and some not so well), but the questions still await philosophic consideration of the ethics of force under different circumstances.

Due process. The paradox of harm and force is further complicated by another line decision found across the system of law enforcement: the argument that not doing harm to those who harm is itself harmful. This is the classic dilemma of "dirty hands"; no matter what the choice is, harm may be done. If a police officer shoots a fleeing suspect, his or her hands are dirtied by hurting the suspect, perhaps unnecessarily. Yet, if the officer does not shoot, his or her hands may be dirtied by the suspect shooting someone else. The problem has been well conceptualized and applied to criminal justice by Carl Klockars (1980), who calls it the "Dirty Harry" problem after the Clint Eastwood movie of that name.

The Dirty Harry problem goes beyond considerations of whether to use legally allowable forms of coercion to stop or prevent harm. It also embraces the question of whether officials should disregard the letter of the law in order to achieve its goals. This includes violating *Miranda* requirements in order to obtain a confession from a murder suspect, conducting illegal searches of persons and places in order to ensure that no weapons are present, and breaking into the homes of suspected spies to plant electronic surveillance equipment. The question may even embrace the entire system of plea bargaining, in which unsophisticated defendants often have little idea of what is happening to them even as they seem to nod agreement in their brief contacts with their attorneys.

Here again, the metaethical issues concerning justice may arise. If due process requirements are to be criticized as unjust (by letting the guilty go free), then it is important to be very clear about the meaning of justice. The balance of probability between false positives and false negatives is also germane, since that is the foundation for the due process requirements. An ample legal literature explores the practical aspects of these questions, especially the exclusionary rule. But other than Klockars' (1980) incisive analysis, the problem awaits philosophical consideration.

Time. Time is a very rich moral dimension of line decisions in law enforcement, as Donald Newman (1978) has demonstrated.

Speedy justice is an ancient norm of Anglo-American culture ("justice delayed is justice denied") and the caseloads of modern urban courts have posed grave practical problems in living up to that norm. Citizens generally want the police to come within minutes of being called, but the backlog of calls (or police taking their time because they view the call as unimportant) often produces delays of over an hour.

Speed is not always a virtue, however. The haste to process the thousands of cases that go through criminal courts each year produces the assembly-line justice which has little room for careful consideration of guilt or innocence. Police officers rushing to the scene of crimes or accidents, or driving in "hot pursuit" of suspects, kill themselves and other citizens hundreds of times each year. Police officers trying to enforce the law without delay may fail to consider options such as negotiation and mediation, thus rushing into shootouts; an example is the Eulia Love case in Los Angeles (Board of Police Commissioners, 1979) in which two police officers confronted a woman brandishing a kitchen knife in a dispute over a utility bill. Rather than avoiding a confrontation and using persuasion, the officers pressed on to create a situation in which they killed the woman in self-defense. Delay and negotiation may also have been a less deadly strategy for dealing with the Attica prison riot in 1971.

In addition to the speed with which tasks are accomplished, there are ethical questions about how to allocate time among different tasks, or whether to perform any tasks at all. The largest time resource in criminal justice is the time police officers spend on preventive patrol, yet that time often weighs heavily on their hands. In the absence of radio calls to respond to, patrol officers do not always have a clear idea of how to spend their time, and waste much of it in idle talk (with each other, not the community). Similarly, judges are often notorious for spending less than half a workday at the bench when their caseload requires little or no preparation, and for taking vacations in the summer when the backlog of cases grows to its largest size of the year. Prosecutors, defense attorneys, and parole officers may have the opposite problem: so little time available for any case that it is difficult, if not impossible, to do a competent job.

Finally, line officials must make some *priorities* among competing tasks in allocating their time. Even patrol officers with only one radio call on a tour of duty cannot spend the entire tour dealing with that call, since they need to be available to take other calls that may come up. A family fight call could take two or three hours to deal with, if an officer decided to mediate the couple's dispute, but few officers give those calls such high priority. If that approach could keep a couple from killing each other (a point on which there is no empirical evidence), then it could deserve the highest priority. Similar problems arise for prosecutors in deciding what cases are worth taking to trial in order to dramatize a particular kind of crime or seek a more severe punishment than plea bargaining could afford.

Rewards. Criminal justice officials are generally underpaid but powerful, a situation that makes it difficult to resist the perquisites, privileges, and gifts the public often offers to them. It also makes it difficult to resist taking possible overtime pay into consideration in making line decisions, such as whether to make an arrest just before the end of a tour of duty, the processing of which will take several more hours. And in any career, there are ethical questions about whether to choose tasks and make decisions that will advance one's career, but not necessarily accomplish the goals of the job itself. Should a police officer make many arrests just to improve his or her chances for promotion to detective? Should a judge give a harsh sentence in a highly publicized case, when he or she has recently given a more lenient sentence in a less publicized case?

The ethical issues in bribery are generally quite straightforward, but in an applied context they become quite muddy. The literature on police corruption (Goldstein, 1975), for example, reveals many rationalizations and defenses police officers construct for taking bribes, or even free meals. "Other people do it." "It's legal for the chief of detectives to eat a free meal when he speaks at a banquet, so why not for me in this coffee shop?" "Gambling doesn't hurt anyone, so it's moral to take money not to enforce laws against it" (clean graft). These rationalizations provide fertile ground for philosophical debate, but written materials of that sort are still lacking.

Loyalty. Line criminal justice officials not only make ethical decisions about their own behavior; they must also decide how to respond to the behavior of their colleagues and supervisors. Loyalty to coworkers is a strong informal norm in many organizations, and a strong ethical argument can be made for that norm under certain conditions. Where workers are ruthlessly exploited and overworked, for example, one might be able to justify lying and covering up for a colleague who is sleeping on duty. That argument is probably made by many police and corrections officers who hold second jobs that exhaust them, although their first jobs do at least guard them against starvation. The question each criminal justice official must face (including judges) is whether they owe more loyalty to their colleagues who break the rules or to the public interest that guides the setting of the rules.

The complexity of this issue should not be underestimated. Students should first be taught to separate their *fear* of informal (or even formal) sanctions for doing something about immoral behavior around them from their sincere and voluntary feelings of *loyalty*, friendship, or trust with the individuals involved. They could then consider the consequences of various courses of action, for their colleagues, themselves, and the public interest, as well as the principles involved: Is it ever right to lie? Suppose no one asks you if your coworkers break rules or laws, is silence justified? Does the decision to be silent or "blow the whistle" depend on the seriousness of the immoral conduct, the extent of personal loyalty to those acting immorally, some other principle, or some combination?

Another issue might be the practical options available for taking action against immoral coworkers. It is impractical, for example, to go to a supervisor to complain about bribery of one's colleagues when the supervisor is also corrupt. It is also impractical to go to the warden of a prison to complain of brutality against prisoners by a guard supervisor if the warden approves of treating prisoners brutally. Access to newspaper reporters, federal prosecutors, and other agents of social control could be considered, along with ethical questions about the order in which the agents should be asked to take action. Perhaps, for example, the warden would not respond as his reputation suggests; perhaps it would be more ethical to give the warden a chance to punish the brutality before going outside to blow the whistle.

This issue is hardly limited to criminal justice, and a growing literature is available as resource material. Sissela Bok's (1978) practical book on lying provides a helpful philosophical context, and a number of books on whistle-blowing (e.g., Peters and Branch, 1972) are available. In criminal justice, the story of Frank Serpico's reaction to corruption in the New York City Police Department

(Maas, 1973) and the story of Tom Murton's discovery of systematic murder in the Arkansas prison system (Murton and Hyams, 1969) have both been made into movies (*Serpico* and *Brubaker*, respectively) and provide good case studies.

b. *Line decisions in each agency*. In addition to the general issues that line officials throughout criminal justice commonly face, there are distinctive ethical issues at each decision point. This list is only a partial inventory; a full list will require the active involvement of many people who have devoted many years of work to the various decision points.

Citizen decisions to report crime. The most common beginning of the entire criminal justice process is a citizen's decision to call the police and report that a crime has occurred. Police discover some crime on their own, but the system basically depends on information volunteered by citizens (Reiss 1971). Citizens are not paid officials of criminal justice, of course, but they were once under a legal obligation in English law to report all crimes and help apprehend the suspects (Melville-Lee, 1901). This legal obligation has withered away, but the ethical obligation may remain. A.M. Rosenthal's book on apathy among New Yorkers, *Thirty-eight Witnesses*, describes the Kitty Genovese case in which thirty-eight people heard a woman scream for help but did nothing while she was being murdered, and provides some good case material on the position of "not wanting to get involved." Even the question of reporting crimes against one's own property or person raises ethical questions, since failure to report impairs police ability to measure, analyze, and respond to crime trends, and generally deter crime.

Police decisions. Police responsibility to detect crime and apprehend suspected criminals can often be accomplished most effectively—or only accomplished at all—in ways that raise substantial ethical questions. The use of tricks and deception in investigation, for example, are central to Bok's (1978) analysis of lying. It is also worth discussing the apparent double standard on this issue. Police officers, for example, don't object to deceiving prostitutes to make arrests, but they sue the police department when its internal affairs unit uses trickery to catch police officers committing crimes (Sherman, 1978). Similarly, congressmen don't always object to the FBI using trickery against radicals and political dissidents, but they may object strongly to the FBI using tricks to catch members of Congress taking bribes (Wilson, 1980). Deception of judges and juries through perjured testimony, another common practice, may seem more obviously unethical because it is illegal, but I have heard police give a spirited ethical defense of the practice.

Tricks and deception raise the additional ethical problem of instigating crime, as distinct from the legal question of whether entrapment—inducing and encouraging someone to commit a crime—has occurred. Providing the opportunity to someone to commit a crime they might not otherwise commit is legal, but the ACLU and others have objected that the method is unethical. The assumption underlying the method is that those who are caught by it are habitual or repetitive offenders, but there are always cases of, for example, sixteen year-old altar boys arrested for taking a wallet from a decoy police officer playing the role of a sleeping, intoxicated derelict. The question of whether the police should "create crime" is a difficult and important one (Marx, 1980).

Police work also poses ethical questions about intruding on the privacy of others through informers, electronic and visual surveillance, and the keeping of dossiers. Whatever a police agency's general practice may be in this regard, each officer should make his or her own moral decision about whether to participate in the practice. Transferring to another unit may not stop the practice or even absolve the officer of any moral obligation to do something about it, but like pacifism, each refusal to participate is a long-term threat to the practice.

Most of the deception issues arise in the context of proactive police work, in which police seek out crimes that citizens do not report. The entire structure of proactive police work raises ethical questions, such as how the targets for investigation should be selected, and how one selection can be justified over another when there is an unknown amount of crime in all walks of life. It is not clear that proactive police methods are, *per se*, any less equitable or less prone to people "playing God" than allocating resources reactively to citizens reports of crime, however (Black, 1973).

Reactive methods also raise questions about how priorities are set among different kinds of crime: are the crimes against rich people given more thorough investigation than crimes against the poor, and if so, does one section of town with almost no crime get half as much patrol coverage as another section of town with fifty times as much serious crime? When a murder suspect is interviewed or interrogated, should high-pressure methods be used to extract a confession? The literature on these questions is only beginning, but a new textbook on police ethics (Elliston and Sherman, forthcoming) will deal with them.

Prosecutors. Perhaps the major ethical issue unique to prosecution is the plea-bargaining process. While most legal scholars have appeared to accept plea bargaining as a necessary evil, some prosecutors have tried to stop it. The attorney general of Alaska, for example, imposed a statewide ban on the practice several years ago (with mixed results—see Anderson, 1979). Whether or not the evil is necessary, however, there has been limited ethical discussion of whether the alleged evil is indeed evil, and if so, why (but see Kipnis, 1976). Nor has there been any analysis, to my knowledge, of how an individual prosecutor caught up in a system that is legal but immoral should deal with his or her situation. We do have Skolnick's (1966) critique and Sudnow's (1965) careful description, but the problem still awaits formal ethical inquiry.

Judges. Judges are also caught up in the plea-bargaining system, almost to the point of having relinquished much of their power to prosecutors in exchange for a speedy flow of cases and the avoidance of backlogs. They must still take the responsibility for the sentences they mete out, however, and that raises the general problem of equity and discretion noted earlier. It also raises the question, virtually unique to judges, of whether they should participate in the "system." A line prosecutor who refused to plea bargain would probably be fired quickly by the chief prosecutor, but judges have long (or lifetime) terms of office to protect them from reprisals. To be sure, they are not immune from pressure, but they probably have more freedom—and responsibility—than many of them would acknowledge. Here again, however, the ethical dilemma lacks any applied philosophical analysis.

Presentence investigators. Probation officers and others who conduct background investigations on convicted criminals prior to their being sentenced face the general problem of insufficient time for their caseload. They also face the unique problem (shared with parole boards) of making predictions about behavior based on the details of a life in a culture and social class quite different from their own. Even those investigators who have come from similar backgrounds to those of the people they investigate—and perhaps especially those upwardly mobile ones—must wrestle with the problem of evaluating poor people by middle-class standards. How much weight should be placed on the fact of parenting an illegitimate child, for example, or of not holding a job for very long? Even if patterns of such behavior correlate well with criminal behavior, the correlation is not perfect and the prediction in an individual case will often be in error. Can the investigator run the risk of a convict being punished according to his lifestyle rather than according to his offense? The broader problem of the goals of criminal justice (discussed below) clearly enters here, but the specific role of the presentence investigator still awaits ethical analysis.

Corrections officers. The unique ethical problems of people working in prisons (and jails, to a lesser extent) arise from the long-term nature of personal relationships with offenders. Police, prosecutors, judges, and presentence investigators rarely see each person they process for more than a few hours at most. But corrections officers may have to live with their charges in the intense environment of a "total institution" (Goffman, 1961) for years at a time. Parole officers also face similar ethical problems in their long-term relations with offenders, although not with the same intensity of daily contact.

A rich sociological literature is available to describe the informal social relationships of the prison, but the ethical problems the descriptions suggest have never been carefully analyzed. Favoritism for some inmates over others and tolerating violence among inmates (to enforce inmate norms) in exchange for generally orderly prison routines are two problems evident in the early literature. More recent times have produced questions such as how much force to use in subduing riots and whether special food should be provided so that Muslim inmates do not violate the dietary laws of their religion. Many of the more recent issues are managerial rather than line decisions, but loyalty questions might then arise for individual officers who believe their prison's policies to be immoral.

c. *Management decisions across the system*. Several ethical decisions for criminal justice managers also cut across the system to a variety of agencies. Three of them seem to attract considerable attention: the many problems associated with the process of policymaking, the specific policies made in the area of affirmative action for recruitment and promotion, and the conflicting loyalties managers face in making supervisory decisions.

Policymaking process. The descriptive literature on criminal justice clearly documents the multiple and often conflicting goals of the criminal justice process: deterrence, retribution, rehabilitation, restitution. The ethical literature also provides substantial analyses of why one of these goals is better than another, and the principles on which criminal justice ought to be based. There is virtually no description or ethical analysis, however, of how a democratic society does or should choose among those goals in its administration of criminal justice.

Is an administrator justified in setting his or her own goals, for example, without consultation with elected officials or community representatives? Not all administrators have that option, of course, but some (like J. Edgar Hoover) have been able to create the independence needed to set their own goals quite explicitly. Others have done the same less openly, fostering certain goals over others in low visibility, day-to-day decisions. In either case, there are important questions about the concentration of ethical decisionmaking for large portions of the system in the hands of one person.

Yet, there are equally important questions about the failure to set any goals at all. The vague-speaking administrator who seeks to avoid setting moral priorities and allows matters to take their own course is probably more common than the arrogant master of bureaucratic power. The police chief whose firearms policy is "leave your gun in the holster until you need to use it"; the administrative judge who does nothing about patterns of grossly inconsistent sentences for the same offenses; the correction commissioner who lets custodial and treatment staff fight over control of the inmates without intervening; all these have made a policy out of having no policy at all.

Herman Goldstein (1977) has clearly presented both the issues and some administrative solutions for a rational and democratic policymaking process for police agencies, and his analysis might apply with minor modifications to courts and corrections. But the nature of the conflicts inherent in the administrative rulemaking solution Goldstein proposes still await philosophical analysis. What principles, for example, should govern a choice between professionally based knowledge about the effectiveness of certain procedures (foot patrol, capital punishment, minimum security prisons) and community beliefs of the opposite viewpoint? What should be done when the dominant values of a community are clearly unethical and violate state law, such as majority public support for police corruption or brutality against blacks? How should community sentiment be measured: through the expressed opinions of activists, through the scientific polling of the entire community, through the votes of elected representatives, or some other method? The memoirs of leading administrators might provide valuable descriptive insight on these and other questions about the ethics of the process by which policy is made, as distinct from the substantive results of that process.

Affirmative action. Police and corrections administrators are frequently challenged for employing, promoting, and retaining disproportionately low numbers of minorities and women, even though civil service systems often give them relatively little discretion over personnel decisions. Both court-ordered and voluntary plans systematically favoring minorities and women have been implemented in some places and resisted in others. The stance the administrators take often seems to be guided by political considerations, which may or may not be proper in a democracy. But the ethical and legal literature on this major issue is growing, and is certainly a stimulating topic for class discussions.

Loyalty and supervision. One of the more difficult aspects of affirmative action cuts across many other administrative issues as well: the degree of obligation an administrator owes to protect the interests of the members of the agency. Many rank-and-file officers (including judges) complain that their administrators do not "back them up" against the various "enemies" of criminal justice: the press, the public, or other sources of criticism. Criminal justice administrators are often sensitive to this charge, especially when they have risen through the ranks in the agency they supervise. Their concern is sociologically understandable in terms of reference group theory. But the question of its moral propriety needs to be carefully examined in the context of specific supervisory practices.

The practices include anything in which supervision might harm the interests of those being supervised. Should a police executive, for example, use "integrity tests," such as the staged dropping of a wallet near a police officer, to measure compliance with procedures? Should an administrative judge establish a procedure for monitoring the hours that trial judges actually spend on the bench? Should a corrections commissioner dismiss a warden who has failed to prevent violence among inmates? Each of these questions rests largely on other principles, such as those governing deception, privacy, and accountability. But for each of them one can also ask whether sympathy for or loyalty to the subordinates who might suffer is a legitimate consideration in making the decision.

There are also specific issues of managerial ethics for each agency, but many of them relate to the line decisions already reviewed. A systematic attempt at listing those issues should await the work of a seminar or other group of managers in each type of criminal justice organization.

B. Research Issues

The ethics of social science research has been subjected to increasing attention in recent years, largely over the questions of the protection of the rights of human subjects and the adequacy of research for making policy decisions (Britell, 1980). But older questions also remain important and should be considered by anyone who devotes a career to criminal justice research: selection of topics, research staff relations, access, and objectivity. Only one of these questions is distinctively concerned with research on criminal justice agencies (and other types of organizations), the problems of objectivity and reciprocity produced by the need to be granted access to the agencies to conduct the research. The others are common to all social science.

1. Access, objectivity and reciprocity

The most direct forms of scientific evidence about the behavior of criminal justice agents (and of criminals in the arms of the law) are "natural" observation and official archives. Both forms of data are under the control of the agencies, and there is usually little a researcher can do to appeal a denial or cutoff of access to the data. Unlike a physicist who is in control of the atoms manipulated in physics research, a criminal justice researcher must bargain with the subject of his or her research. These bargains for access raise two ethical problems: objectivity and reciprocity.

Scientists are morally bound by their professions to be objective in describing what they observe. When they observe officials engaged in misconduct, racial discrimination, or simply a failure to do their job, objective description may obviously embarrass the organization being studied. Some organizations may only allow access on the condition that nothing be published without the approval of the agency head. If these are the only terms under which a researcher can study an important problem, it is ethical to accept them? How are the principles of objectivity and the need to contribute to knowledge reconciled? Is incomplete description, as opposed to inaccurate description, morally better than no description at all?

On the other hand, there are ethical questions about the right of a social scientist to go around intruding on other people's privacy, using up the resources of a public organization to advance a scientific career, possibly delaying the regular work of the agency, and providing little useful knowledge to the agency in return. What are the moral obligations of researchers to the agencies they study? Should they combine the scientist's role with the management consultant's? Should they delay sharing the findings of research with the agency until the findings are ready for publication, or should they offer to meet with agency officials as soon as the findings are in? Should they ever break a promise not to publish findings without agency approval? To my knowledge, there is no ethical literature on these questions, although there are some good descriptions of the relationships involved (e.g., Manning, 1976).

2. Selection of Topics

Access issues may also affect a scientist's objectivity in the selection of topics to be studied, although here the nature of "objectivity" is rather different. As Weber (1948) argued, the primary role of values in social science ought to be the guidance of selecting topics. Both access and funding priorities may distort this process of guidance, diverting scientists from topics their values tell them are important to topics for which they can obtain agency access and financial support. No one gives scientists a monopoly on true values, however, and in a democratic society it *may* be better to have priorities for social research determined by funding agencies rather than by scientists as individuals—assuming that (a) the priority setting is not dominated by certain class interests or the goal of social repression, and that (b) the setting of priorities in this fashion does not stifle scientific creativity and serendipity (Merton, 1968). But these assumptions are highly debatable, and they deserve empirical examination to develop a valid ethical analysis.

3. Human subjects

The protection of the rights of human subjects of research first became an ethical issue in biomedical research. With a few exceptions, such as the controversy over the deception used in Milgram's (1974) research on obedience to authority, the issue was imposed on social science by administrative fiat. The literature on human subjects in social research that has appeared since federal regulations were imposed has generally focused on the question of whether there ought to be such regulations, and if so, how they should be fashioned and administered (e.g., Klockars and O'Connor, 1979). Although the ethical decisions this issue forces individual researchers to confront are relatively straightforward—for example, whether or not to obey the regulations—their practical significance alone suggests that they be carefully considered in the graduate education of criminal justice researchers.

4. Research staff relations

A final question of applied ethics for social science research is what principles should govern relationships among the members of a research team. The norm of collegiality dominates the rhetoric of science, but hierarchy is present everywhere. Problems arise when the hierarchy of research authority and the hierarchy of contribution to the research effort do not match. Different members may see the hierarchy of contributions differently, of course. The senior author may write the research design, supervise data collection and analysis, write the final report, and still spend less time on the project than any other member of the research team. Research assistants commonly resent the senior authorship of the project director and argue that the senior author's credit is unethical. On the other hand, some project directors do simply put their names on reports that they have done little to produce.

These relations pose practical questions that desperately need ethical analysis. How much credit should a senior researcher receive after conceptualizing a research design, writing a grant proposal and obtaining funding, and hiring a project director to conduct the research. None? Second authorship? Can standard weights be assigned to contributions, or is each case unique? What principles should be applied?

Or, as another example, does a salaried research assistant who does nothing but collect data, run the computer, and discuss the findings with the project director deserve equal or second authorship, a footnote, or no acknowledgment? The American Sociological Association's proposed code of ethics requires written agreement on these matters at the outset of a research project, but that still does not provide any answers on how they ought to be resolved.

C. Teaching Issues

There is little about the ethics of teaching criminal justice that is distinctive or different from the teaching of any other subject in higher education. Criminal justice professors may be under somewhat more pressure from external sources than other liberal arts professors to teach a practical curriculum (Sherman, et al., 1978), but they also face the common dilemmas of entertainment to keep enrollment up versus rigor in teaching, devoting enough time to class preparation for good teaching while still publishing enough not to perish, and responding helpfully to the unpreparedness of new college students without lowering academic standards.

There may be, however, a distinctive ethical issue in the teaching of ethics (whether implicitly or explicitly) in criminal justice: the problem of indoctrination.* While it is true that all ethics teachers must face this issue (Hastings Center, 1980), the consequences of indoctrination in criminal justice teaching could make the problem especially significant in this field. For a criminal justice teacher to indoctrinate students in values supporting the use of excessive force against rude suspects or offenders, the practice of "minor" corruption, the importance of vengeance as a goal for criminal justice, or other values contrary to the spirit or letter of our laws could reinforce existing immoral practices. The connection between teaching and behavior, to be sure, is tenuous at most, but even if one criminal justice agent were to derive justification for immoral practice from a criminal justice course it could be a life or death matter. It is equally improper to indoctrinate students in a liberal point of view about criminal justice, of course, rather than working toward the student's ability to dispense with the teacher for moral reasoning. Present or future teachers should be helped to reason for themselves that any form of indoctrination is improper. They should also be able to recognize it wherever they find it, including indoctrination in their own value systems.

Few graduate programs in social science or humanities formally address any aspect of college teaching, let alone the ethics of teaching. Given the central role of ethics in the subject matter of criminal justice, it is especially important that this gap be filled in the doctoral program.

*The Hastings Center Report (1980: 59) defines indoctrination as "a systematic attempt to persuade students of the validity of a belief system, one that (a) radically rules out the possibility of accepting other belief systems; (b) in a deliberate fashion, involves withholding from students either serious objections to that system or those tools of analysis that would enable the student to see its flaws; (c) excludes the possibility of rejection of the belief system; and (d) penalizes deviation." Most important, indoctrination rules out the logical and self-critical processes under which a belief system might be rejected.

V. Ethical Frameworks

Identifying ethical issues is obviously only the first step toward teaching and scholarship. In most institutions it is probably the only step (if any) that is taken. Students learn that there is a difference of opinion and are left to make up their minds individually, according to their own values. The problem with that approach is that thinking clearly and rigorously about ethics is not just a matter of applying preexisting personal values. Instead, it requires an analysis of both relevant facts and values within a coherent ethical framework of principles and premises.

The application of formal ethical frameworks to criminal justice issues will make the teaching of ethics explicit and serious. It may scare away some students and make ethics harder to teach, but it will challenge the minds of both teachers and students who attempt it. Most of all, it will demonstrate that all moral reasoning implies a framework of analysis, but that it is very difficult to construct and employ a coherent and consistent framework.

A. The Variety of Frameworks

1. Rejected Frameworks

The experimental police ethics course at SUNY-Albany began with an introduction to the modern ethical frameworks still widely in use. In retrospect, this may have been a mistake, for it only encouraged the view that all frameworks are equal; what you decide depends on the framework you choose, and your choice is simply a matter of taste or personal values. A good way to discourage this view would be to begin the presentation of ethical frameworks with some widely rejected examples (Rosen and Caplan, 1980:39). By showing that a framework can be internally consistent and yet lead to abhorrent decisions, this method emphasizes very early on that the selection of an ethical framework is a very serious business.

The most dramatic rejected ethical frameworks to use for this purpose are *naturalism* and *evolutionism* (or social Darwinism). The naturalist principle that might makes right, that those who can dominate others should do so, can clearly be linked to the official philosophy and practices of Nazi Germany. So can the even more pernicious doctrine that only the fittest and strongest should survive in order to speed the evolution of the human race more rapidly toward perfection. Examples of moral decisions that can be derived from these frameworks, such as sterilizing all those people whose IQ score is below 100, should provide clues to the kinds of principles—such as the dignity of persons—that should be included in a valid ethical framework.

Students can also be taught the failure of other ethical frameworks by applying them to criminal justice examples. *Subjectivism*, or justifying each person making a moral decision on the grounds of what he or she believes to be right, is probably a good descriptive ethical framework for the exercise of discretion in criminal justice. Yet that is precisely what is wrong with it. Subjectivism applied to those decisions conflicts with other principles students should accept, such as equality before the law. It also makes a mockery of all administrative policy, thus reducing the effectiveness of criminal justice at accomplishing its ethically justified goals.

Egoism also offers two principles that can be rejected quite convincingly (Frankena, 1973:18): "(1) that an individual's one and only basic obligation is to promote for himself the greatest possible balance of good over evil," and "(2) that even in making second- and third-person moral judgments an individual should go by what is to *his own* advantage." The exclusive self-love that dictates these principles can lead to disastrous consequences if universalized. If police officers and judges wanted to be perfectly safe, they would never antagonize dangerous criminals by arresting them or sentencing them to prison. With ethical egoism as the moral basis of criminal justice, the system would cease to function.

Finally, *ethical relativism* can be rejected, if not as easily as the others. The notion that "what is right or good for one individual or society is not right or good for another, even if the situations involved are similar" (Frankena, 1973:109), has wide appeal, especially to people raised to value tolerance. But since its basic premise is that there is no one moral truth, the approach denies that ethics are possible. In that sense, relativism is not an ethical framework at all.

The presentation of rejected ethical frameworks can be tied together with the argument that they fail to represent a "moral point of view." Baier (1966) defines this viewpoint as not being egoistic, doing things on principle, being willing to universalize the principles, and considering the good of everyone alike. None of the rejected frameworks meet these conditions, but the modern frameworks do.

2. Modern Frameworks

Four modern ethical frameworks are used most frequently in modern ethical discussion, even though two of them are more than a century old: utilitarianism, Kant's ethics, Sartre's existentialism, and Rawls's theory of justice. All four share certain principles, and the same ethical conclusion can often be derived from more than one framework. But the differences among them are important, both substantively and as a way of demonstrating the methodology of ethical analysis.

Utilitarianism is the most common ethical framework for debates over criminal justice issues, as well as in American public policy discussion in general (Fleishman and Payne, 1980:53). More specifically, one form of utilitarianism, called "rule-utilitarianism," is frequently employed: the principle that we ought to act according to rules that are determined according to what will promote the greatest general good for everyone. We should always execute murderers, according to this framework, if scientific evidence shows that more lives will be saved through the deterrent effect of executions than will be lost from the executions themselves. John Stuart Mill's *Utilitarianism*, while not clearly rule-utilitarianism (as distinct from "act-utilitarianism, or acting in each situation according to the consequences of greatest good regardless of what the consequences of that action would be if adopted as a general rule"), provides a widely used original text for the general utilitarian framework.

Utilitarianism is a prime example of what philosophers call *teleological* theories, or ethical frameworks that lead to choices on the basis of the consequences of those choices. In contrast to this consequentialist approach are three versions of "*deontological*" (or nonteleological) ethics, all of which hold that other aspects of a decision besides the nature of its consequences may make it right or wrong. Deontological theory holds that actions or rules may be morally right even if they do not produce the greatest good for the greatest number (Frankena, 1973:15). One well-known deontological framework is Immanuel Kant's theory of ethics, best introduced in his *Foundations of the Metaphysics of Morals*. Another is Jean Paul Sartre's existentialism, best represented in his *Existentialism and Humanism*. The most widely discussed new ethical theory of recent years seems to be John Rawls's *A Theory of Justice* (1971), a rule-deontological theory that, like Kant's theory, proceeds from the premise of a social contract binding individuals together in their own interests rather than the premise of utilities for society as a whole.

B. Choosing among Frameworks

The most difficult problem in the study and teaching of ethics is the process of choice among competing ethical frameworks. While Rawls's theory may seem most convincing, for example, it is hard to be sure that choice is based on anything more than subjectivism. Since no one has been able to demonstrate an intellectually acceptable method of choosing ethical frameworks, it is clearly difficult to do with a class.

The Hastings Center project addressed this problem in *Ethics in the Undergraduate Curriculum* (Rosen and Caplan, 1980:36-40). The discussion is helpful, but like all such discussions it is necessarily unsatisfactory (p. 38):

> . . . there is the inevitable disagreement among students about which normative theory is correct. One student will be a Kantian, another an egoist, and a third a utilitarian. The teacher at this point *must* make a decision. . . . Mere disagreement bogs down, almost always, because students lack a means of working it out. The teacher has to supply the means, and failure to supply it conveys, usually, the message that there is no framework, and that the selection of a normative theory is arbitrary or a matter of taste.

It is clear that the teacher must make a decision. The problem is how to make it. It is relatively easy to reject theories founded on principles (like might makes right) that we consensually view as immoral, but how does one choose between, say, utilitarianism and Rawls? What procedure can be used that evaluates the two theories and comes to a conclusion while still avoiding the danger of indoctrination?

Yet, the problem must be muddled through. As Frederick Elliston (1980) points out, a teacher who avoids taking a position may teach a position he or she does not intend: that there is no position. Merely playing the devil's advocate, skeptically attacking all moral theories, is probably poor pedagogy as well as poor substance. At the level of specific decisions, it may even be appropriate to use different frameworks for different kinds of decision. But it is still a very fine line to walk between the perils of indoctrination and the frustrations of indecision.

C. Professional Codes of Ethics

Ethical theories are not the only conceptual frameworks that can be applied to specific moral choices. Many of the professional associations related to criminal justice have developed what might be interpreted as applied ethical frameworks, more traditionally known as codes of ethics. Since many criminal justice students will be bound by one or several of those codes, it is worthwhile considering their adequacy as a guide to moral decisionmaking in occupational settings. A list of the addresses from which copies of the codes of ethics may be obtained is included here as an appendix.

The inescapable conclusion about any of these codes is that

they are not sufficient guides to decisionmaking, no more than the Ten Commandments or other relatively simple lists of prohibitions and proscriptions. All of what they say may be good and true, but they usually lack clear principles to apply to a broad range of situations. In that sense, they do not satisfy Baier's (1965) definition of the "moral point of view."

The Canons of Police Ethics of the International Association of Chiefs of Police, for example, covers eleven aspects of the law enforcement officer's job: primary responsibility, limits of authority, familiarity with the law, the proper means to achieve ends, cooperation with other public officials, private conduct, conduct toward the public, conduct toward law violators, gifts and favors, presentation of evidence, and attitude toward the profession. Aside from being a rather unsystematic hodge-podge of disparate issues, the IACP canons provide little clear guidance for many of the central ethical issues in police work. The canons are silent on the crucial questions of discretion, time, and loyalty. The canons do require that officers conduct themselves in "such a manner as will minimize the possibility of having to use force," but that still leaves the crucial ethical question of when to use force unanswered. It is clear on the question of gifts from outsiders (forbidden), but silent on the more complex aspects of rewards noted earlier. The canons offer neither specific rules for most problems nor general principles that could be applied to specific problems.

At the opposite end of the spectrum from vagueness to specificity is the American Bar Association's Model Code of Professional Responsibility. Recently revised, the code contains nine succinct canons with finely detailed "Ethical Considerations" and specific rules punishable by discipline attached to each canon. This method almost approaches casuistry, the seventeenth-century philosophical practice of making long lists of situations with injunctions of what to do in each of them. The canon that a lawyer should represent a client competently, for example, is followed by an ethical consideration that a "lawyer should not seek, by contract or other means, to limit his individual liability to his client for his malpractice," and a disciplinary rule to the same effect. The problem with this kind of approach, as Kelly (1980:37) notes, is that it encourages law students to approach their ethics courses with the goal of learning "how far a lawyer can go legally before being subjected to the risk of discipline or trouble."

Perhaps the weakness of the professional codes reflects the absence of serious scholarship on the applied ethical issues of criminal justice professions. It may also reflect uncertainty about the purpose of such codes. Whatever the reason, it is unlikely that students will derive much moral guidance from the codes.

A criminal justice teacher may also want to consider the value of codes of ethics for a system in which most agents are already bound by a complex set of administrative rules and policies. The discussion could consider the view that professional ethics grew out of an attempt to make money-earning respectable by imposing the gentleman's values on those of the tradesman (Lieberman, 1970). It could also consider the argument that detailed codes of ethics have hindered more than helped the quality of professional service. The potential value of code as a pressure device for changing unethical administrative rules might also be discussed. A basic point should be that if codes of ethics are to be used at all, they should be taken seriously. That is not the current situation in most criminal justice agencies.

VI. Teaching Issues for Ethics

Ethical issues in criminal justice cannot, of course, be taught simply by listing the scope of the moral problems and bringing various ethical frameworks to bear upon them. While that is basically what this monograph proposes, the approach must be implemented very carefully, paying close attention to the major teaching issues. An ethics course in criminal justice may otherwise run the risk of failure. Once the problem of "fitting ethics in" to the curriculum (chapter III) has been solved, the most critical teaching issues are who shall teach, diverse student backgrounds, reading materials, course organization, methods of instruction, and student evaluation.

A. Who Shall Teach?

The most critical teaching issue for ethics in criminal justice is the virtual absence of people qualified to do it. Many criminal justice professors may feel qualified to teach ethics, but as The Hastings Center Report (1980:63) argues, they are probably mistaken:

> . . . good training in the technical aspects [of a subject] . . . does not automatically confer any special skill in analyzing or resolving the moral dilemmas arising in those fields. It is seductive to think they do. Most thoughtful practitioners will have wrestled with moral problems, will have discussed them with colleagues, and may well in their undergraduate education, or in their efforts in self-education, have given some thought to ethical theory and analysis. That,

however, is not sufficient for teaching a course in ethics—anymore than the personal experience of having balanced a checkbook and the daily perusal of the financial section of the newspaper qualifies one to teach a course in economics.

Three options for competent teaching are available, each of which satisfies the recommendation of The Hastings Center Report that applied ethics teaching be truly interdisciplinary, combining technical and ethical expertise. One option, perhaps the most practical in an era of declining resources, is for criminal justice faculty to acquire the equivalent of one year of graduate training in moral philosophy or theology. The training should make them adequately grounded in the language, concepts, modes of analysis, and standards for distinguishing good work from bad in ethics. Whether this requires a certain number of specific courses or can be accomplished entirely through self-directed readings will depend on the individual.

Another option is for faculty members with doctorates in moral philosophy or theology to acquire technical competence in criminal justice issues. Here again, either the first year of a Ph.D. program in criminal justice or a program of independent study supplemented by field observation would seem to provide an adequate grounding. The major problem with this approach is that criminal justice departments seem to be very reluctant to hire trained philosophers, and many of them now have no available positions to put philosophers in, even if the department was willing.

A third option may be particularly attractive to academic administrators facing declining enrollments in the liberal arts: team-teaching combining members of the philosophy and criminal justice departments. The advantages of instant expertise and a stimulating give-and-take are clear. The disadvantages are the possible personality clashes between instructors, the extra expense, the fight over the academic accounting of the enrollments (which department claims them?), and the danger of teaching the material in a simple, side-by-side manner without integrating ethics and criminal justice (Hastings Center, 1980:65-66). For those departments willing to move quickly into an ethics course, however, team-teaching may be the best solution.

In the long run, a program of fellowships, or at least summer workshops, for both philosophers and criminal justice professors would be the best way to provide both competent teaching and scholarship on ethics in criminal justice. But the need is too great to wait for government or foundation funding for such a large-scale undertaking.

B. Diverse Student Backgrounds

Criminal justice classes typically enroll students from a wide variety of backgrounds. Some have many years of experience in criminal justice whereas others have none. Some have broad intellectual appetites whereas others are interested only in the practical problems of doing criminal justice work. Some are open-minded and tolerant, whereas others are strongly wedded to narrow positions. Some are sympathetic to the plight of suspects, defendants, and inmates, whereas others are more concerned about the stresses on the criminal justice official.

This diversity is an asset from the standpoint of class discussion. It virtually guarantees that there will be different opinions on any moral question. It also guarantees that some students will be able to contribute a true case study out of experience. But the diversity also poses problems.

Where ethics is a required course, the diverse backgrounds will produce varying levels of interest. This problem can be particularly difficult when the ethical frameworks are introduced, often baffling even the most interested students. Perhaps the best way to deal with uninterested students is to involve them in discussion as much as possible, fighting their disinterest with Socratic questioning. This kind of attention is both an art and a potentially serious sanction and must be handled with care. But with time it should usually be possible to persuade a student that ethical analysis is worthwhile.

Where ethics is not a required course, uninterested students are likely to stay away. But even the interested students will vary in their ability to keep up with a discussion. It is advisable, then, to stop at regular intervals, summarize what has been said and the key points of difference, before proceeding on to the next issue. Blackboard charts of reasoning steps might aide this process. Uninterrupted discussion otherwise jumps around from premises to principles to conclusions without the logical steps being laid out in an orderly fashion.

C. Reading Materials

The most important problem produced by diversity is the selection of reading materials. Some students are capable of and interested in reading the original texts of the major moral philosophers, whereas others find the idea unattractive. The student evaluations of the experimental SUNY-Albany police ethics course showed great difference of opinion on this point, as well as general dissatisfaction with one of the more widely used introductory ethics textbooks, Frankena (1973).

More important than the diversity of student reactions to reading materials, however, is the general absence of the right kind of materials. The SUNY-Albany evaluations showed that students wanted readings that combined ethical problems in the way we did in class. Aside from Klockars' (1980) paper on the "Dirty Harry Problem," however, we were unable to locate materials of this kind.

The absence of integrated readings is simply the other side of the lack of scholarship on applied ethical issues in criminal justice, which is, in turn, produced by the absence of a community of scholars trained in the interdisciplinary skills needed to analyze these issues. The cyclical nature of the problem is frustrating, for the lack of scholars is the result of the lack of demand for them to teach courses. Once the courses get going (if they ever do), even with inadequate reading materials, better materials should follow. In the meantime, there are many useful readings already mentioned that can help serve as a basis for discussion.

D. Course Organization

The lack of reading materials compounds an already difficult problem of organizing courses on criminal justice ethics. The central difficulty of course organization is that the readings fail to provide integration of practical issues and ethical frameworks.

There are at least two standard ways to organize any applied ethics course (Fleishman and Payne, 1980). One is to begin with the value conflicts present in concrete occupational situations. The other is to begin with the ethical principles and frameworks used to analyze the situations. The advantage of the first approach is that you immediately capture students' interest with the fascinating dilemmas of real life, rather than boring them with seemingly pointless abstract terms and procedures. The advantage of the second approach is that when the discussion turns to concrete situations the students are already prepared with the tools of ethical analysis, thus improving the quality of the discussion.*

A third approach might be to begin with a practical problem, present all the relevant facts, discuss the issue, and criticize the discussion for lacking coherence and guiding principles. The four ethical frameworks could then be introduced by way of application to the problem already introduced. This format would both lend a concrete grounding to the frameworks and show the need to use frameworks for coherent ethical analysis.

No matter how the frameworks are introduced, there is still the problem of what to do for the rest of the course. One danger is a steady diet of dilemmas, which might push students into "thoroughgoing relativism," as it seems to do in some legal ethics courses (Kelly, 1980:28). Discussion of one problem after another needs to be relieved with a variety of teaching methods. There should also be some sense of direction in the course, so that students feel they are not simply swallowing the whole landscape but actually getting to some place new—a new way of thinking, of understanding, or even of action.

Most important is the need to come back to the frameworks to evaluate them in the light of criminal justice issues. The SUNY-Albany police ethics course often became too involved in discussing the details of a practical problem and ran out of time before the problem could be attacked with the various frameworks. Indeed, a general shortcoming of the case method is that students seek more facts and get distracted by nonethical issues (Hastings Center, 1980:69-70). Learning from that lesson, it seems important to insure that all the frameworks are aired. Perhaps a good

*Philosophy Professor Jeffrey Reiman of the American University School of Justice can provide syllabi following both approaches.

conclusion to the course would be to deal with the question of choosing frameworks, deciding which framework is the most adequate and appropriate for criminal justice.

E. Methods of Instruction

The teaching of ethics is amenable to many different methods, as a study of methods used in journalism ethics classes found (Christians and Covert, 1980:17): lectures, case studies, small subgroup discussion, student presentations of their own topics, lectures by outside professionals, in-depth study of a few selected issues, panels (or debates) of opposing viewpoints, student reports on interviews with professionals, films, audio and video tapes, slides and transparencies, lectures by academics from other departments, role-playing, simulation games, novels, plays, clippings, and photographs. While using all these methods in a one-term course would probably exhaust both the students and the instructor, there is much to be said for using a variety of methods.

Each method provides a different way of experiencing ethical issues and analysis. Many of the nonlecture methods call for active participation in a decision process, thwarting the tendency of many students to avoid making difficult ethical decisions. The more dramatic methods help stimulate emotional involvement in the ethical issues, one of the major goals suggested earlier, and by preserving lectures for a small percentage of the classes, such as the explanation and evaluation of moral frameworks, the impact of each lecture may be increased.

The SUNY-Albany police ethics course used three methods beyond the relatively rare lectures: decision scenarios, debates, and small group discussions. The decision scenarios were case studies with very little information presented in them, for example:

> It is 1:30 A.M. in a white residential neighborhood. While on routine patrol, you observed a black man, about thirty years of age, dressed in dungarees and sneakers. Should you stop and ask him for identification?

The arguments for and against stopping were then considered within the four major ethical frameworks. Sometimes the scenarios were tied into the small group discussions with each group assigned a different framework.

The scenarios were well rated in the course evaluation, but not the small group discussions. The groups failed to develop good leadership, and discussion often flagged. Those who disliked the framework assigned to their group found it uncomfortable to use that perspective.

Our solution was to move to a heavy reliance on debate, since debates contained both of the other methods: focused on moral assertions ("there are no conditions under which police officers should go on strike for more pay"), the small groups held discussions to prepare for the public encounter. To add incentive to the preparation, we pronounced a winning team at the end of each debate, and gave reasons for the decision.

The debates were stimulating and kept the class focused on the ethical issues. The major requirement for winning was to weave the substantive discussion into an ethical framework and use it to support the position. But since the position was already assigned, this procedure may have denigrated the ethical frameworks, giving students the impression that they are simply tools for argument to be manipulated according to a predetermined conclusion, much like the cases cited in a lawyer's brief. That was not our intention, but it may have been the result.

A better method for exercising analytical skills might be the technique of "moral negotiation" (Rosen and Caplan, 1980:49–50), developed at Ohio State University. This technique begins by clarifying and specifying a moral issue (which often serves to resolve any differences of opinion). The next step is to list all the reasons for each side of the issue, reducing them to two conditional statements, such as:

1. If capital punishment:
   a. fails to deter homicide,
   b. tends to reduce respect for human life, and
   c. violates the dignity of persons, then
   d. capital punishment is unethical.

2. If capital punishment
   a. reduces homicide rates,
   b. does not reduce respect for human life,
   c. does not violate the bodily dignity of persons, then
   d. capital punishment is justified.

This listing of both facts and principles on which the conclusion rests focuses the points of disagreement. It is often the case that insufficient facts are available for a final decision. But if the facts can be assumed through a "conditional agreement" for purposes of analysis, then the analysis can move into the ethical principles at stake. It may be that students of different views agree on the principles and merely disagree on the facts—or vice versa. This method provides an effective way to determine very quickly just what the differences may be (see also Rosen's [1978] *Strategies of Ethics*).

F. Student Evaluation

The evaluation of student performance in an ethics course and student evaluation of the course itself both pose distinctive problems related to the goals of the course. The traditional student performance measures of classroom observation, papers, and private discussions measure moral imagination, the ability to recognize moral issues, the development of analytic skills, the sense of moral obligation, and the student's stance toward disagreement and ambiguity. The traditional measures can probably give some clues, but not as well as they measure the retention and comprehension of a defined body of information. If it were not for the danger that ethics might not be taken seriously, it would be preferable to offer it as a nongraded course (with mandatory attendance).

Rosen and Caplan (1980:28-29) suggest three nontraditional measures of student performance, two of which strike me as too intrusive: peer interviews and observation outside the classroom, both to gather evidence about how students may have changed in relation to the course goals. Gathering this sort of subjective evidence on individuals without careful attention to the nature and motives of the persons supplying the information is very dangerous, because it raises ethical problems of its own about the privacy of students and confidentiality of data. The third method, testing the level of individuals' moral reasoning, may be a poor way to measure the accomplishment of some of the goals, but at least it operates equally on all students with their knowledge and implicit consent.

Student evaluations of an ethics course (as distinct from evaluating the teacher) should probably be an anonymous self-assessment of whether the goals described earlier were realized for them as individuals. A follow-up survey some years later of the same students might provide a useful perspective on how long the effects of an ethics course can "last," or how much time must pass before students make the connections to real life. Course evaluations should also ask about the apparent value of the teaching methods and course organization, thus providing useful feedback on the suggestions made earlier.

VII Conclusion

Higher education in criminal justice is at a turning point. It has come to the end of its rapid early growth, and has already witnessed declining enrollments in some areas. The adjustment to a new level of operation, whatever that may be, will be painful. But it will also provide an opportunity for reconsideration of the curriculum—an opportunity for building in the explicit consideration of ethics.

As more committees are appointed to review the curriculum and, perhaps, design new courses, they should find several of the other publications in the Hastings Center series to be helpful. Although much work remains to be done in the scholarship on ethical issues in criminal justice, the resources on applied ethics teaching in general are quite plentiful—more than enough for a curriculum review committee to read and evaluate, and enough for a professor designing a new course to borrow ideas for application to criminal justice.

Two trends in criminal justice may contribute to the adoption of ethics courses. One is the changing character of the faculty. According to the most recent survey of criminal justice faculty qualifications conducted by the Joint Commission on Criminal Justice and Criminology Education and Standards, the percentage of professors with graduate degrees and doctorates has increased substantially since the last such survey was undertaken. This trend toward an apparently younger, more highly educated faculty with less criminal justice practitioner experience could admittedly have mixed results. On the one hand, it could make collective faculty values and priorities more scientistic, and more resistant to allegedly "soft" subjects such as ethics. On the other hand, a better-educated faculty should be more open-minded than the traditional ex-police faculty members, and less threatened by the introduction of ethical tools and concepts or people who are expert in them. If our graduate schools do anything, they should train people to recognize the merits of a rational argument—including the argument for building-in the explicit teaching of ethics.

The other trend is a part of the broader changes in society which prompted The Hastings Center Report on *The Teaching of Ethics in Higher Education*: an apparent increase in concern about ethics in the workplace. While many college freshmen were barely old enough in 1972–74 to understand the Watergate affair, their interest in the morals of work has clearly been heightened by the social and legislative changes flowing in the wake of Watergate: the Foreign Corrupt Practices Act, Abscam, "Koreagate," the rise of whistle-blowing, and the spread of "investigative reporting" exposés. If for no other reason than a prudent desire not to get caught up in a scandal, college students appear to be highly sensitive to these issues. Their interest can easily translate into both enrollments (making criminal justice ethics courses feasible) and active intellectual interest (making them academically rewarding and worthwhile).

It is worth noting that police academies also appear to be showing more interest in teaching ethics as part of basic training, at least as measured by informal discussions. The FBI Academy Library has received an increasing number of requests for curricular materials on police ethics. A continuing program of summer workshops for police academy instructors at Boston University, now several years old, has reached many academies around the country. The active interest of criminal justice agencies may provide yet another source of support for the growth of teaching ethics in college-level criminal justice programs.

In sum, the prospects for more explicit teaching of ethics in criminal justice may be equal to the need for it. Even if the prospects were grim, it would still be a goal worth pursuing. No other issue has blocked communication between academics and practitioners in criminal justice more than latent disagreements over ethics. If the differences could be brought out in the open for more rational examination, then both justice and the criminal justice system would be well served.

Finally, a brief summary of the argument may be helpful:

1. There is a serious need for teaching and research on the applied ethics of criminal justice.
2. Courses on those issues can be easily adapted to virtually all levels and kinds of criminal justice issues.
3. The goals of such courses ought to include stimulating the moral imagination, developing skills in the recognition and analysis of ethical issues, eliciting a sense of moral obligation, fostering the ability to tolerate—and resist—disagreement and ambiguity, understanding the morality of coercion, integrating technical and moral competence, and becoming familiar with the full range of moral issues in criminology and criminal justice.
4. The scope of ethical issues is broad, but courses should teach students how to deal with the issues generally rather than what is right for each issue.
5. Some formal ethical framework is necessary for a rigorous analysis of any difficult ethical problem.
6. Professional codes of ethics provide little guidance, creating an even greater need for teaching formal ethical frameworks.
7. Any effort to establish an ethics course should give careful consideration to the unique teaching issues for ethics.

Bibliography

Anderson, David. "You Can't Cop a Plea in Alaska Any More," *Police Magazine*, January 1979, pp. 4–14.

Baier, Kurt (1966). *The Moral Point of View: A Rational Basis of Ethics*. New York: Random House.

Baum, Robert J. (1980). *Ethics and Engineering Curricula*. Hastings-on-Hudson, N.Y.: The Hastings Center.

Black, Donald J. (1973). "The Mobilization of Law," *Journal of Legal Studies*, vol. 1.

Board of Police Commissioners, City of Los Angeles (1979). *Report on the Killing of Eulia Love*.

Bok, Sissela (1978). *Lying: Moral Choice in Public and Private Life*. New York.: Pantheon.

Bouza, Anthony V. Statement presented to the National Advisory Commission on Higher Education for Police Officers, John Jay College, June 20, 1977

Britell, Jenne K. (1980). "Hazards in Social Research," *New York Times*, Sept. 7, p. 18, education section.

Carnegie Foundation for the Advancement of Teaching (1977). *Missions of the College Curriculum*. San Francisco: Jossey-Bass.

Christians, Clifford G. and Catherine L. Covert (1980). *Teaching Ethics in Journalism Education*. Hastings-on-Hudson, N.Y.: The Hastings Center.

Clouser, K. Danner (1980). *Teaching Bioethics: Strategies, Problems, and Resources*. Hastings-on-Hudson, N.Y.: The Hastings Center.

Elliston, Frederick (1979). "Deadly Force." Paper Presented at Temple University.

———(1980). "Teaching Police Ethics." Paper Presented at Vassar College.

Fleishman, Joel L. and Bruce L. Payne (1980). *Ethical Dilemmas and the Education of Policymakers*. Hastings-on-Hudson, N.Y.: The Hastings Center.

Frankena, William K. (1973). *Ethics*. 2nd ed. Englewood Cliffs, N.J.: Prentice-Hall.

Goffman, Erving (1961). *Asylums*. New York: Anchor Books.

Goldstein, Herman (1977). *Policing a Free Society*. Cambridge, Mass.: Ballinger.

———(1975). *Police Corruption*. Washington, D.C.: Police Foundation.

Gouldner, Alvin (1962). "Anti-Minotaur: The Myth of a Value-Free Sociology," *Social Problems*, vol. 9, pp. 199–213.

Gusfield, Joseph R. (1966). *Symbolic Crusade: Status Politics and the American Temperance Movement*. Champaign-Urbana, Ill.: University of Illinois Press.

Hastings Center (1980). *The Teaching of Ethics in Higher Education*. Hastings-on-Hudson, N.Y.: The Hastings Center.

Hoover, Larry T. (1976). *Police Educational Characteristics and Curricula*. Washington, D.C.: U.S.G.P.O.

Kant, Immanuel (1959). *Foundations of the Metaphysics of Morals*. Indianapolis, Ind.: Bobbs-Merrill.

Kelly, Michael J. (1980). *Legal Ethics and Legal Education*. Hastings-on-Hudson, N.Y.: Hastings Center.

Kipnis, Kenneth. "Criminal Justice and the Negotiated Plea." *Ethics*, January, 1976.

Klockars, Carl B. and Finbarr W. O'Connor (1979). *Deviance and Decency: The Ethics of Research with Human Subjects*. Beverly Hills, Calif.: Sage Publishing Co.

Klockars, Carl B. (1980). "The Dirty Harry Problem," *Annals of the American Academy of Political and Social Science,* vol. 452, November 1980.

Kohlberg, Lawrence (1976). "Moral Stages and Moralization," in Thomas Lickona, ed., *Moral Development and Behavior*. New York: Holt, Rinehart and Winston.

Lieberman, Jethro K. (1970). *The Tyranny of the Experts: How Professionals are Closing the Open Society*. New York: Walker.

Maas, Peter (1973). *Serpico*. New York: Viking.

Manning, P. (1976). "The Researcher: An Alien in the Police World." In A. Niederhoffer and A. S. Blumberg, eds., *The Ambivalent Force: Perspectives on Police.*. Hinsdale, Ill: Dryden Press.

Marx, Gary T. (1980). "The New Police Undercover Work," *Urban Life*. vol. 8, no. 4 (January), pp. 399–46.

Matza, David (1969). *Becoming Deviant*. Englewood Cliffs, N.J.: Prentice-Hall.

Melville-Lee, W.A. (1901). *A History of Police in England.* Montclair, N.J.: Patterson Smith Reprint

Merton, Robert K. (1968). *Social Theory and Social Structure*. New York: Free Press.

Milgram, Stanley. (1974). *Obedience to Authority: An Experimental View*. New York: Harper & Row.

Mill, John Stuart (1976). *Utilitarianism*. Cleveland, Ohio: Collins-World.

Morris, Norval and Gordon Hawkins (1970). *The Honest Politician's Guide to Crime Control*. Chicago: University of Chicago Press.

Muir, William Ker, Jr. (1977). *Police: Streetcorner Politicians*. Chicago: University of Chicago Press.

Murton, Tom and Joe Hyams (1969). *Accomplices to the Crime: The Arkansas Prison Scandal*. New York.: Grove Press.

Newman, Donald J. (1978). *Introduction to Criminal Justice*. 2nd ed. Philadelphia: J. B. Lippincott.

Packer, Herbert (1968). *The Limits of the Criminal Sanction*. Palo Alto, Calif.: Stanford University Press.

Peters, Charles and Taylor Branch (1972). *Blowing the Whistle*. New York: Praeger.

Pipkin, Ronald M. (1979). "Law School Instruction in Professional Responsibility: A Curricular Paradox." *American Bar Foundation Research Journal*, no. 2.

Police Foundation (1979). *Higher Education for Police Officers: A Symposium*. Washington, D.C.: The Police Foundation.

Powers, Charles W. and David Vogel (1980). *Ethics in the Education of Business Managers*. Hastings-on-Hudson, N.Y.: The Hastings Center.

Rawls, John (1971). *A Theory of Justice*. Cambridge, Mass.: Harvard University Press.

Reiman, Jeffery H. (1979). "Research Subjects, Political Subjects, and Human Subjects," pp. 35–57 in Klockars and O'Connor, 1979.

Reiss, Albert J., Jr. (1971) *The Police and the Public*. New Haven: Yale University Press.

Reiss, Albert J., Jr. (1980) "Controlling Police Use of Deadly Force." *Annals of the American Academy of Political and Social Science*. vol. 452, November.

Reppetto, Thomas A. (1979) "Remarks." *Proceedings of the National Symposium on Higher Education for Police Officers*. Washington, D.C.: Police Foundation.

Rosen, Bernard (1978). *Strategies of Ethics*. Boston, Mass.: Houghton-Mifflin.

Rosen, Bernard and Arthur L. Caplan (1980). *Ethics in the Undergraduate Curriculum*. Hastings-on-Hudson, N.Y.: The Hastings Center.

Rosenthal, Abraham M. (1964). *Thirty-eight Witnesses*. New York: McGraw-Hill.

Sartre, Jean-Paul (1977). *Existentialism and Humanism*. Brooklyn, N.Y.: Haskell.

Sellin, Thorsten (1938). *Culture Conflict and Crime*. Millwood, N.Y.: Kraus Reprint.

Sherman, Lawrence W. and The National Advisory Commission on Higher Education for Police Officers (1978). *The Quality of Police Education: A Critical Review with Recommendations for Improving Programs in Higher Education*. San Francisco, Calif.: Jossey-Bass.

Sherman, L. W. and Mark Blumberg (1981). "Higher Education and Police Use of Deadly Force." *Journal of Criminal Justice*, vol. 9: 317–31.

Sherman L. W. (1980a). "Causes of Police Behavior: The Current State of Quantitative Research," *Journal of Research in Crime and Delinquency*.

———. (1980b). "Execution Without Trial: Police Homicide and the Constitution," *Vanderbilt Law Review*, 33:71.

Simon, Sidney B., Leland Howe, and Howard Kirschenbaum (1972). *Values Clarification: A Handbook of Practical Strategies for Teachers and Students*. New York: Hart.

Skolnick, Jerome (1966). *Justice Without Trial: Law Enforcement in a Democratic Society*. 2nd ed. New York: Wiley.

Sloan, Douglas (1980). "The Teaching of Ethics in the American Undergraduate Curriculum, 1876–1976," in Daniel Callahan and Sissela Bok, eds., *Ethics Teaching in Higher Education*, pp. 1–57. New York: Plenum Press.

Strickland, Jeanne L. "Committee Wants to Make Ethics Required Learning Fare," *John Jay Journalist*, June 1, 1980.

Sudnow, David (1965). "Normal Crimes: Sociological Features of the Penal Code in a Public Defender's Office," *Social Problems*, vol. 12, pp. 255–76.

Walton, Paul, Ian Taylor, and Jock Young (1973). *The New Criminology*. London: Routledge and Kegan Paul.

Warwick, Donald P. (1980). *The Teaching of Ethics in the Social Sciences*. Hastings-on-Hudson, N.Y.: The Hastings Center.

Weber, Max (1948). "Science as a Vocation," in H. H. Gerth and C. Wright Mills, ed. and trans. from *Max Weber: Essays in Sociology*, New York: Free Press.

Weber, Max (1964). *Max Weber: The Theory of Social and Economic Organization*, trans. and ed. A.M. Henderson and Talcott Parsons. New York: Free Press.

Westley, William (1970). *Violence and the Police: A Sociological Study of Law, Custom, and Morality*. Cambridge, Mass.: MIT Press.

Wilson, James Q. (1980). "The Changing FBI: The Road to Abscam," *The Public Interest*, 59 (Spring) pp. 3–14.

Appendix

Addresses for Obtaining Professional Codes of Ethics Relevant to Criminal Justice

American Bar Association
1800 M Street, N.W., Suite 200
Washington, D.C. 20006
(202) 331–2200

American Correctional Association
4321 Hartwick Road
College Park, MD
(301) 864–1070

American Political Science Association
1527 New Hampshire Avenue, N.W.
Washington, D.C.
(202) 483–2512

American Psychological Association
1200 - 17th Street, N.W.
Washington, D.C.
(202) 296–3224

American Sociological
Association
1722 N Street, N.W.
Washington, D.C. 20006
(202) 833–3410

International Association of
Chiefs of Police
11 Firstfield Road
Gaithersburg, MD
(301) 948–0922

National Association of Social
Workers
1425 H Street, N.W.
Washington, D.C. 20006
(202) 628–6800

National Conference of
Christians and Jews
2041 Martin Luther King, Jr.
Ave., S.E.
Washington, D.C.
(202) 678–9400

United Nations Information
Center
2101 L Street, N.W.
Washington, D.C. 20006
(202) 296–0822

DATE DUE

~~8/5/82~~			
~~5/19/83~~			
~~NOV 2 2 1985~~			
~~APR 6 1987~~			
~~MAR 1 6 1994~~			